MY JOURNEY HOMEWARD

My Journey Homeward

Walter Trobisch

SERVANT BOOKS
Ann Arbor, Michigan

Cover design by Michael P. Andaloro

Vine Books is an imprint of Servant Publications
especially designed to serve Evangelical Christians

Published by Servant Books
P.O. Box 8617
Ann Arbor, Michigan 48107

Printed in the United States of America
ISBN 0-89283-299-1

86 87 88 89 90   10 9 8 7 6 5 4 3 2 1

Dedication

This book is dedicated to all those couples who caught the vision of "couple-power" and who, through the example of their own family life, are spreading the message throughout the world.

Contents

Foreword

WALTER TROBISCH WAS BORN IN LEIPZIG, GERMANY, on November 29, 1923. He had a deep experience of faith during the dark days of World War II when serving as an infantry soldier on the Russian front. Through a miracle of God he survived the Battle of Stalingrad. Severely wounded, he was brought to Vienna, Austria. During his period of convalescence, he began his studies in theology at the university there.

It was during this period of time that he began sending monthly letters to his Christian youth group in Leipzig, his hometown. In them, he combined a meditation on a biblical text with his own observations and experiences. Already then he knew that "communication is strength."

In 1948-49, after completing his theological examinations at the University of Heidelberg, he was one of the first German foreign exchange students to come to the United States. While studying at Augustana Seminary in Rock Island, Illinois, he met my mother, Ingrid Hult. They were married in Mannheim, Germany, in 1952, and a year later they became pioneer missionaries in northern Cameroun, West Africa, sent out under the auspices of the American Lutheran Church.

During his time in Cameroun, he wrote his first book, *I Loved a Girl,* which was soon translated into many languages and reached millions of readers throughout the world. Overnight he became a much sought after speaker. He was asked for new answers to theological, medical, social, and political questions about marriage and family problems in the developing countries of the Third World. A flood of readers' letters reached him, coming not only from Africa but also from Europe, Asia, and the United States. The problems which the book dealt with were international.

In 1963, my parents came home from Africa with their five children. After a few months' furlough in the United States, they found a home for their family in the foothills of the Austrian Alps. Here they could spend most of their time answering the letters they received from readers asking for spiritual help and practical advice regarding family problems. They were supported financially and spiritually in this ministry by praying friends and church groups.

From the first days of World War II until the end of his life, Walter Trobisch continued his practice of writing regularly to his friends. It seemed that he was often "pregnant" with one of these *Rundbriefe* (circular letters), as he called them, and then he was absentminded and introversive. He would then disappear into his study, and a few hours later he would come out with the handwritten pages which had generous margins for my mother's questions and corrections.

This volume contains selections from those letters which were written from 1967 until the time of my father's death in 1979. Beginning usually with a meditation on the Scripture theme for the month, the themes of the letters are varied; they cover the landmarks of life, birth, death, marriage, and divorce. He writes about other customs and countries, about pastoral care and psychotherapy; he interprets the words of poets as well as exposes critical conditions and practices. Meditative passages stand next to objective analyses and personal explanations.

One cannot understand Walter Trobisch aright as only a theorist and systematist, and although he was a fascinating speaker, his real gift was the gift of *Seelsorge* (soul care). He never looked upon marriage and family counseling as an end in itself. Rather, it was the "landing strip" for the Gospel, as he once called it.

I enjoyed discussing theological questions with him. We were not always in agreement on every point—to be expected between father and son and between two different generations of theologians—yet I always felt a great admiration for the integrity of his views. They were always embedded deep in his own life, and he seems to have made no important decision without a profound wrestling in his heart.

On October 13, 1979, at the age of fifty-five, Walter Trobisch died unexpectedly from a heart attack. These letters to his friends belong to the most personal and timeless writings which he left us.

David Trobisch, Instructor
Department of Theology,
University of Heidelberg, Germany

Acknowledgements

"Communication is strength," they say, but it also takes strength and teamwork to communicate. I want to thank those whose teamwork made this book possible:

My oldest daughter, Katrine Stewart, who wrote the Afterword—a letter she composed for our family and friends two weeks after her father's death.

My second son, David, who did all the groundwork in preparing the German edition of the manuscript.

My third son, Stephen, who through long hours and dogged determination translated the German text into English when I was on a trip to Africa last summer.

My friends and editors, Elisabeth Wetter of Brockhaus Verlag in Germany, whose master touch brought the right order into the book; Ann Spangler and Mary Case of Servant Publications whose practical advice and constant encouragement brought this English edition to birth.

And a warm thanks to my "circle of lovers" and praying friends who held up my arms when they were growing faint.

—Ingrid Trobisch

A Word at the Beginning
We Don't Know What Is Coming

IT IS HARD TO PUT INTO WORDS what has moved us so deeply of late! We feel strongly that we are living through an unbelievable period of time, the end of an old and the beginning of a new epoch. The full impact of this age cannot yet be seen. Our only certainty is that far-reaching changes are on the way, and they will affect all of us.

Like earthquakes, whose tremors unite subterraneously, so the whole world trembles. The great unrest of youth, acts of terrorism, wars that don't end—they are all somehow connected.

Yet everything that is being said and written to describe and characterize this new unrest, to give it a name and even explain why it is happening, is being said and written prematurely. All that we can do right now is to be wide awake and to listen silently. Something is coming that we can't yet recognize. We need to hang on to the watchword: "We don't know what is coming, but we do know who is coming."

One thing we know for sure: in this new, possibly last, period of history, He wants to come to us. The only thing we really have in this hour is the prayer: "Let me know your way, so that I may know you."

When we look at all that is happening around us, our personal lives seem so insignificant and unimportant. Yet the word "me" is still in this prayer quoted above. We can only recognize and meet him in our personal lives as we walk the path of his individual guidance. Only through recognizing and meeting him in this way can healing power be released—power that is effective in this day of weak faith and that shows, in spite of everything, that God himself is the beginning, the middle, and the end of all history and of each epoch in our individual lives.

—Walter Trobisch

Part One

Experience and Promise

1

No Room in the Inn
Easter 1975

Place Is Life

A PLACE WAS THE FIRST GIFT of God to man. "And the Lord God planted a garden . . . and there he placed the man whom he had formed" (Gn 2:8).

There is perhaps nothing which causes us more suffering than the loss of the God-given "Garden" while we are living here as a part of the fallen world. We are in need of both place and space. The Bible uses the same word for both terms.

A child will suffer if he is deprived of having his own place. He needs at least a corner of a room, a shelf, or a drawer that is completely his own and where he can keep his treasures. But he also needs a place where he can sometimes be alone. One of our children found that in her Austrian boarding school, the only place she could find solitude was under a dark velvet cover which protected the grand piano in the music room.

As adults we also struggle continuously to find both place and space. To be deprived of it means to be deprived of life. In our talks with married couples, this problem comes up again and again. Often the fact is simply overlooked that a wife and mother also needs her own place, at least her own desk. In our spiritual lives, the lack of a place for a quiet time with God is one of our greatest practical difficulties. Jesus, too, lacked a place in this world: "Foxes have holes and birds of the air have nests; but the Son of Man has nowhere to lay his head" (Lk 9:58). God himself suffered.

No Room in the Inn

"...because there was no room for them in the inn" (Lk 2:7).

This verse can be applied to both Christmas and Good Friday. The world has no room for its Creator. It refuses to let God enter its inn and puts him instead into a manger. It expels him as a strange, disturbing body and nails him to the cross.

The manger and the cross were the only places the world had left over for God. Those who live with God will share in God's lack of a place, which means suffering. This suffering will increase even more as the world approaches its end. Think, for example, of the persecutions in Russia, China, Cambodia, Vietnam, South Africa, Ethiopia. No power of this world will protect the Christians' place, which gets smaller and smaller. Are we conscious of the fact that we are in the midst of a dangerous battle? When will it be our turn? Are we ready?

Make Room by Making Order

This is the challenge of the hour: to make room by making order. Maybe we should begin by straightening up the things we can see—our drawers, shelves, closets, and also our finances. But above all, we must make order inwardly.

To make order creates new space, but we also need space in which to make order. In a small room where things are heaped up one on top of the other so that we cannot even turn around, we cannot make order. To turn to God takes room as well. Our greatest danger is that we might lose this room needed to turn around and to repent. We may miss the chance just as Esau did: "He was rejected, for he found no place (no room) to repent, though he sought it with tears" (Heb 12:17).

Place Is Grace

This place needed for repentance is not at our disposal. God has to grant it. God wants to give it to us. The servant reports, "and still there is room" (Lk 14:22) at God's great banquet table to which all of us are invited. To Moses, who longed to see God's glory, the Lord said, "Behold, there is a place by me" (Ex 33:21). Then God put Moses in the cleft of the rock and covered him with his hand.

The cleft is the place of grace. Hemmed in by the narrow walls of rock—here is God's place for us in this world.

God's Place in the "Non-Place" of the World

God's place in the inn was the stable and the manger. God's place in the world is the cross.

Do we understand the signs of the time?

We suffer in knowing that God has no place in this world. At the same time, we see another dimension opening up, one which is both unexpected and unthinkable. The skies open above the stable of Bethlehem.

"Where there is no way, God's ways begin." The non-place of the world becomes God's place.

"Enlarge the place of your tent" (Is 54:2). A tent is a place with restricted space. How can it be enlarged?

Just as the heavens enlarged the stable of Bethlehem, so the narrowness and limited quantity of place is broken through by an unlimited quality of space. God's space breaks into the non-place of the world. The place of our tent is enlarged. In the midst of a hopeless situation, in the narrow cleft, we experience wideness and freedom, room in which to breathe, both space and place.

David, persecuted by Saul and hunted like a wounded deer, gave this testimony, "Thou hast set my feet in a broad place" (Ps 31:8).

God Himself Is Our Place

This is the meaning of the biblical expression: "to be in the Lord," "to be in Christ." It is like being in a room. The narrow torture cell—the most horrible non-place in the world—is so narrow that one cannot lie down, but one always falls against a wall. Jesus can be the wall against which we fall. Our room is exactly as large as he is close to us. He is our tent, our place which continuously grows larger, where we find space to breathe and where we can even become place and space for others.

Becoming a Place in Space

Since the space age we are more conscious of unlimited space in our universe. Unlimited space can be just as frightening to us as a very narrow place in a closetlike room.

Jesus Christ is the answer to both. Instead of causing fear and claustrophobia in limited space, he shelters us.

Instead of causing menace and threat in unlimited space, he sets us free.

Jesus Christ alone can teach us the secret: not to seek shelter but to give shelter. Not to seek a place and space but to give place and space. To become a home—a place for others. This brings us to the message of Easter.

Our Place in God's Inn

The last place the world had to give to Jesus was the grave. However, here too he had "no room in the inn." His was a borrowed grave, but the grave couldn't hold him. Because of the resurrection, this word of suffering—"no room in the inn"—receives new meaning. It conveys hope. Jesus bursts the boundaries of any place and space in this world to prepare place and space for us in eternity (Jn 14:2). He himself is my place and space. Unrestricted by any power of this world, Jesus Christ is our place in God's inn.

2

How to Know the Will of God

KNOWING GOD'S WILL in certain life situations is the biggest problem of most Christians. Knowing God's will is a necessity for making the right decisions. To know is an art. God himself has to teach this art to us. "Lord, teach me...."

There are Christians who have learned the art of letting God guide them. There are others who don't even have antennae for seeking God's guidance. Knowing God's will is not the problem, but living as a Christian without even searching for or experiencing God's guidance is.

We want to share three experiences which might be of help:

When we returned from our trip to Australia, we had exactly three weeks to prepare for our next trip to Nigeria. We desperately needed that time to rest, to be with our family, and to catch up with our mail. Among the letters on our desk we found an invitation for both of us to Cali, Colombia, to attend the first international conference for leaders and teachers in the worldwide movement of natural family planning.

Considering the circumstances, our first reaction was: No! Ingrid wrote a letter that very same evening declining the invitation. The next morning she awakened early and said, "I have no peace. I feel it was wrong to write that letter. This is a very important meeting, and one of us should attend. Maybe you and Ruth can go ahead to Nigeria, and I will meet you there after attending the conference in Cali."

We decided to take a concrete step in this direction. We called the International Federation for Family Life Promotion in Washington, which had invited us. They promised to send us an air ticket for Ingrid. Everything was reserved for her coming. They were also in agreement with her return trip via Nigeria. Ingrid laid down the receiver and said, "Now I'm at peace."

The first experience: Often guidance will become clear when we take a concrete step in a certain direction. All at once a still, small voice speaks to us gently in our hearts and we know: "I am going in the right direction," or, "This step is wrong." According to 1 Kings 19:12, the Lord was not in the strong wind, nor the earthquake, nor the fire—all very dramatic occurrences—but he spoke in a sound of gentle stillness. This sound cannot be heard from the outside. Only those who have an inner antenna and who stop and listen in their quiet time will be able to know God's guidance. This is the art.

The second experience: If the inner antennae have received the message, then you must follow it through without looking to the left or right, without paying attention to the way the wind blows. "He who observes the wind [and waits for all conditions to be favorable] will not sow; and he who regards the clouds will not reap" (Eccl 11:4). The outward circumstances are always ambiguous and can only be interpreted correctly in the light of the still, small voice. This sign which is outside of our control is infallible.

It is like the needle of a compass that shows us the direction we should take. Or like the commands given from the control tower when a plane is landing. We can hear a small voice telling us: "This is not right for you. Hands off." Or we hear: "This is a good opportunity for you. Try it."

We did carry out this daring plan and went through this tunnel of unusual guidance. Ingrid arrived in Lagos, Nigeria, after attending the IFFLP conference in South America, on the same day that Ruth and I arrived there from Austria. We held our seminar for thirty-five Lutheran pastors and their wives, with the help of our African co-workers, Jean and Ernestine Banyolak. Ingrid and Ruth returned home by way of Cameroun and Chad.

After the seminar, I sent Jean and Ernestine to Bouaké,

Ivory Coast, to the first All-African Conference for Evangelical Christians to be held there. The theme was "The Christian Family," and I thought it well if an African couple would be the ones to give these messages instead of me.

As my airplane took off from Lagos, I suddenly had the feeling this step was wrong. When I landed in Salzburg ten hours later, I still had this feeling: "I shouldn't be here, I'm in the wrong place." When I got home I found a letter from Bouaké which underlined this feeling. It contained an urgent and repeated invitation, together with a check for my travel expenses and the program of the conference. I discovered that it was not a question of only one lecture as I had anticipated, but they had given me four of the morning sessions of a six-day conference.

I knew at once that this would be too much of a burden for Jean and Ernestine. On the spot, I decided to fly back to Africa. I arrived at the conference grounds exactly half an hour before my first lecture was to begin, just enough time to have prayer with Jean and Ernestine and plan our teamwork. Right on time, all three of us stood on the platform.

The third experience: The art of letting oneself be guided also includes the readiness to be corrected. This is a very humiliating experience to admit in front of God, in front of oneself, and in front of others: I made a mistake. I was wrong. Significantly enough in Psalm 119:67 and 71, we read twice about "humiliation." "Before I was afflicted [humiliated], I went astray" (verse 67). "It was good for me that I was afflicted [humiliated], that I might learn thy statutes" (verse 71). To accept humiliation is part of the learning process in the art of finding God's guidance.

To perceive and then to decide: God does not show us the whole way but only the next step when we are in eye contact with him. His promise: "I will counsel you with my eye upon you" (Ps 32:8).

3

Depression

AS WE GO FROM PLACE TO PLACE, we are struck over and over again by the many depressed Christians we meet. They do not lack faith or spiritual depth. They are sincere believers, living in close fellowship with the Lord, and yet again and again they have to struggle with depressions. (We certainly do not exclude ourselves from among them.)

At the root of every depression is the feeling of having lost something: disappointment is caused by the loss of hope, bereavement by the loss of a loved one, loneliness by the loss of fellowship. There is an age depression—a loss of youth; a retirement depression—loss of work; a moving depression—loss of one's four walls, one's place where one felt at home. And there are the countless depressive moods for which it is difficult to find a reason, except for the general feeling of losing out on life, of losing oneself, of wasting away.

The Bible, that tremendously human book, understands our feelings. The one who prayed Psalm 31, for instance, certainly knew what depressions are:

I am in distress;
my eye is wasted away from grief,
my soul and my body also.
For my life is spent with sorrow,
and my years with sighing;
my strength fails because of my misery,
and my bones waste away. (Ps 31:9, 10)

This feeling: I am spent, consumed, eaten up. I am becoming less and less. I am vanishing away. What psychosomatic medicine discovers today, the psalmist experienced long ago—grief of the soul means grief of the body.

I am ... a horror to my neighbors,
... those who see me in the street flee from me.
Yea, I hear the whispering of many ...
as they scheme together against me.... (Ps 31:11, 13)

This feeling: everyone is against me, nobody understands me, accepts me, loves me. I am hopelessly alone.

I have passed out of mind like one who is dead;
I have become like a broken vessel. (Ps 31:12)

This feeling: I cannot contain myself, hold myself together. I am running out. Everything is flowing out of me. I am losing, losing, losing.

Many men of great faith have had depressions: the apostle Paul, Martin Luther, the Danish theologian Søren Kirkegaard, the French philosopher Blaise Pascal, the Russian poet Fëdor Dostoevski—to mention only a few. All of them were sincere Christians.

Martin Luther made the following suggestions to fight depressions:

1. Avoid being alone and seek fellowship with others who generate joy.

2. Listen to music or make music. "Go away, devil, I have to sing and play now to my Lord Jesus."

3. Refuse to get engaged in a battle with heavy and depressing thoughts.

4. Rely upon the promises of Scripture.

5. Praise and give thanks as David did in Psalm 103: "Bless the Lord, O my soul; and forget none of his benefits."

6. Seek and accept the consolation offered you by others. (You cannot lift yourself out of a swamp by grasping your own hair.)

A friend of ours has a depression emergency kit, written down like a doctor's prescription because when she is depressed, she may not be able to recall it herself. She picks out a special promise from Bible verses prepared just for this occasion. Then she makes herself a good cup of tea, and as she drinks it she listens to her favorite record. She also has an absorbing book which she longs to read but which she has saved for this depression. Afterwards she calls up a friend and combines the visit to her with a walk in the fresh air.

However, we should not look at depression as something negative only. We were deeply comforted ourselves when one of our counselors told us, "All people of worth and value have depressions." There is something like a capacity to be depressed. It takes a certain inner substance and depth of mind to be able to have depressions. Shallow, superficial people seldom have depressions. It is much easier for them simply to cut the thread of life, for, as the philosopher Landsberg puts it, "Often a man kills himself because he is unable to despair."

The poet Owlglass reports this conversation between two friends:

"Why are you so depressed, my friend?" asks one of them.

"I wish I could fly away and leave all my burdens behind me," answers the other. "I am so full of them and so heavyhearted because of them. Why can't I be lighthearted?"

"Why are you not empty-hearted?" responds the first one.

If you could have the choice, which would you rather be: lighthearted and empty—or heavyhearted and full? The German word for depression is *Schwermut,* which means literally "the courage to be heavyhearted." We can rejoice in depression because we are filled and not empty. Through the burdens entrusted to us, the loving hands of God work in us and upon us.

4

Is God Real?

LATELY WE HAVE HAD A NUMBER OF TALKS and some correspondence with people whose faith has broken apart. Their belief in the God of love and righteousness is indeed tested severely because of all the problems for which no solution can be found in our world.

Nobody seems to be able to stop the terrible things happening all around us. The old questions which we had in Germany during the nights of bombing are re-awakened: "How could God let this happen?" "Why, if he is the God of love, doesn't he make use of his power?" When we look at people who are helpless and defenseless against injustice, we ask, "Where is God's righteousness?"

People who ask these questions are the same ones who take God seriously. They are not those who like to form discussion and demonstration groups, but they are the ones who fight in silence and remain unseen. Only the person who believes can doubt.

It is good to remember that these questions are far older than our problems. They are as old as mankind and are expressed throughout the Bible.

In many psalms (as in Psalm 73) and most of all in the book of Job, these questions are raised harshly and angrily. Even Jesus was asked them again and again by his disciples: John 9:1-3; Luke 13:1-5; Luke 24:19-21. It really helps to look up the answers Jesus gives in these verses. They are deep and enlightening even though they never wholly satisfy our human way of thinking. Our logic is not able to classify them systematically, and those who believe have to accept that fact. They would have to agree with the psalmist when he says, "But when I thought how to understand this, it seemed to me a wearisome task" (Ps 73:16).

Someone said to us once: "Since I no longer picture God as real, everything has become easier for me." Yes, indeed; to believe is not "simple" in the sense that things are simplified. Faith does not avoid reasoning, but it stands up under it. Faith lives through this strain and suffering. It is important to have a faith that is stronger than our feeling: "Nevertheless I am continually with thee" (Ps 73:23).

No one of us, however, is fully secure with this "in spite of everything—faith." We never have faith as a safe possession in our pockets. Only if we repeatedly fight for it from one crisis to another will faith remain alive. To hide under a false security blanket of "total faith" is no alternative. In reality, that is nothing but running away from having to think. Such a state of total belief is sterile. The ones who suffer in crises and the ones who fight certainly have a better understanding of the reality of the living God than the "total" believer who is dead sure.

For this reason it may be very helpful to the insecure and doubting to know that the Bible discriminates between rejecting the Word and doubting it, between the denial of God and the failure of faith, between renouncing and temptation.

Paul writes (2 Tm 2:12), "If we deny him, he also will deny us." Logically, he should continue, "If we are unfaithful, he will also be unfaithful to us." Exactly this, however, God will not do. On the contrary, "If we are faithless, he remains faithful—for he cannot deny himself" (2 Tm 2:13). Luther's translation says, "If we are faithless, he abideth faithful."

Someone wrote to us in their struggle of not being able to believe: "I don't believe in him. But does he still believe in me from the very beginning? That would be wonderful! The gift of dumbfounded, childish belief in the gospel is given to the struggling and not to the secure. God's faith is not dependent on our belief."

Who is able to believe the unbelievable?

5

In the World You Have Anxiety

THE SECRET THEME OF THE HOUR is not the energy crisis but anxiety. Young people have anxiety about the unpredictability of their futures. Older people are afraid of another economic depression and another war, things which they've already suffered through. Young and old, the low and the mighty, are all gripped by anxiety and fear.

During World War II when I was trapped behind the front lines in the battle of Stalingrad, I wrote a newsletter to my youth group in Leipzig which began with the simple sentence: "I am afraid." Admitting this at a time when we were all trained to be heroic broke all the rules.

It is so good that the Lord does not ask us to do spiritual chin-ups. He doesn't try to talk us out of fear or advise us to repress it. I don't need to say, "I am afraid, but I really shouldn't have that feeling." I am free to say soberly, "In the world you have anxiety." This is just the way it is. Because Jesus said this to his disciples, it means simply for us, "You may be a child of God and yet be fearful." This means liberation from all the tenseness, the chin-ups, which we could only stand for a short time anyway. We don't need to be fearful of fear. We can even admit to ourselves that we are fearful.

We must learn how to live with fear. Jesus' word is very helpful: "In the world you have tribulation; but take courage, I have overcome the world" (Jn 16:33). The Greek word for "tribulation" contains the idea of "being pressured," "being trapped." The German translation uses the word *Angst*. It comes from *enge* and means "strait," "narrowness," being in a tight spot, in a bottleneck, zeroed in on. All these expressions describe the experience of fear.

We cannot attack fear directly but only indirectly according to the rule of the "knight's move" in chess. The knight is not allowed to attack his opponent straight-on but only "around the corner." In the same way, we can only deal with fear "around the corner" in an act of surrender to the one who has overcome the world. Jesus didn't say, "I have overcome anxiety" but, "I have overcome the world." "We are afflicted in every way, but not crushed; perplexed, but not driven to despair" (2 Cor 4:8). The one who overcame the world also had fear.

That is why in spite of everything, in the midst of our anxiety, we hear the words "do not be afraid" not as a challenge but as a gift. We no longer need to have fear of fear.

6

Seek the Kingdom of God!

B UT SEEK FIRST HIS KINGDOM and his righteousness, and all these things shall be yours as well" (Mt 6:33).

To seek: This points out the direction of the vision. We must keep in eye contact with it and not be sidetracked.

We must be singleminded in following our very personal calling.

First: This means to establish priorities, to differentiate the important from the unimportant, to fight daily for the gift of being able to say no to temptations and things which would divert, hinder, or disturb us from our calling.

Kingdom of God: This is the incomprehensible Reality behind all comprehensible reality. Ricarda Huch tries to point this out with the following words: "God is not in the invisible; not in the visible; but He is in the effect upon the visible." No organization nor institution has completely grasped this reality—and yet we make use of earthly vessels, of the incarnation. We can never completely escape the tension which Luther describes in one of his Christmas songs: "The one misunderstood by all the world lies in Mary's lap."

His righteousness: This is the righteousness of the cross, of the one who was unjustly condemned by the world. The one who was cast out, who was a failure, who did not succeed, and yet who—mysterious tension—in surrendering becomes the only real power in the world. This power penetrates and puts leaven into everything. Just through his surrender he becomes a spring that will never dry up.

To seek the Kingdom of God and his righteousness means to partake of this tension. On the one hand, it means immense freedom: being free from things, from human organizations, from being bound to securities and that which we can put our hands on. The experience of fear in the human heart, however, is strongly connected to this experience of freedom: the fear of the unknown, the fear of being insecure, and, along with this, the fear of being troubled. This is why the words are added to the command: "Seek . . . and then all these things shall be yours as well."

All these things: This certainly does not only mean food and clothing but also a full life with everything that belongs to it, including humor, a laugh that sets us free. First of all, the power and the skill to endure this tension are necessary; without that the Kingdom of God and his righteousness cannot be experienced. It is the direction of the vision which always accompanies our calling.

7

Setting Out for a New Land

AT THE BEGINNING OF EACH NEW MARRIAGE SEMINAR, we have to cope with despondency and hopelessness. We have to realize we can not build upon our past experiences. Each new ministry is like setting out for a new land. We must get ready for departure; we must get ready for the immediate situation and the concrete needs which are placed into our hands.

God keeps on shouting to us that we should go out to the summit, and he challenges us to new waters that we never dared to conquer before.

If we take a look at our own strength next to the

greatness of God's commands, we stand forlorn. "But at your bidding I will let down the nets" (Lk 5:5). When we look back on what, at the time, seemed a road full of curves, we realize that from God's perspective everything went straight and we thankfully acknowledge, "I know that thou canst do all things, and that no purpose of thine can be thwarted" (Jb 42:2).

This insight is most often only given to us in looking back. When walking we are not always aware of this. Some of the steps seem too hard for us. At every fork of the road, we have to struggle again with the question of what is according to his plan. Being in such a struggle, we prefer to be silent rather than to speak or even to write, but every once in a while we have to step out in order to point out a specific need.

So many times we are asked how we survive financially. Since we have given up a steady income, the answer is short and simple: the more we help, the more we are helped.

We are asked: When will we go back to Africa? Who will eventually carry on our work? We don't know the answers; we only know one thing: "I know that Thou canst do all things, and that no purpose of thine can be thwarted" (Jb 42:2).

8

The Sixth Commandment and the New Morality

"I FIND MY DELIGHT IN THY COMMANDMENTS, which I love" (Ps 119:47). A common belief today is that only the one who does not let himself be limited by God's commandments can be a happy and independent person, that he who does delight in God's commandments will miss out on life and become neurotic and sick.

The Psalmist contradicts this belief: "I find my delight in thy commandments, which I love."

I remember a very heated discussion in our Leipzig youth group in 1940 about the film *I Accuse*. This film depicted how a doctor killed his terminally ill wife with a drug overdose. Being accused of murder, he defended himself with the sentence: "I loved my wife." This film questioned the validity of the fifth commandment for the sake of love. At that time, this film was used to psychologically prepare the Germans for the murdering of the terminally ill by the Nazi S.S. forces.

Today—for the sake of "love"—the validity of the sixth commandment is questioned. The "old" morality of a pre-Christian Africa and the "new" morality of a post-Christian Europe shake hands.

The falling of one commandment causes all the others to fall with it. Love and God's commandment never exclude each other. This is difficult to comprehend with our human rationality. In your particular situation, for example, your human rationality may see the giving of your self outside of or before marriage as a beautiful lie, a soft murder, an expression of love. When picturing your life as a whole, it always looks different.

Jesus says, "If you love *me*, you will keep my commandments" (Jn 14:15). Me! This is more than merely being humanitarian. Only the one who loves obeys, and only the one who obeys loves. This obedience is no "golden cage" but the only way to freedom.

"I find my delight in thy commandments, which I love."

9

Water of Life

"AND LET HIM WHO IS THIRSTY COME, let him who desires take the water of life without cost" (Rv 22:17).

This sounds so simple! Just like a recipe: "Take..." As if it would be that simple!

We are suspicious of offers like this. "Whoever desires, let him come. . . ." It resembles a television commercial convincing us that we only need to take the right thing at the right moment in order to reach the goal of our choice.

Recently in Mannheim, Germany, billboards were put up proclaiming this message: "Whoever wants to stay young should buy a carpet." Apart from the impossibility of staying young, it is hard to imagine how a carpet, of all things, could accomplish this. In spite of that, maybe someone will try it.

Too often we are disappointed and have bad experiences with such offers. Somewhere there is always a catch, especially if you don't have to pay for it! For example, our son David naïvely filled out a questionnaire which came in the mail. He was surprised when a bill came. The questionnaire had said "free" on it, but that only meant the postage was free for sending in the order.

In the *Three Penny Opera* of Bertolt Brecht it says, "Unfortunately one has never heard that something was good and then it really turned out to be!" Where is the catch in our Bible verse? There is none unless we put one there ourselves. A catch is often a temptation to which we open the door if we separate God's offer from its real meaning.

Thirsting but Not Coming

First of all, it is possible to be thirsty and yet not come. To have a yearning desire in the heart but not to take the water of life which is offered here. Other springs seem to be more attractive, even though in the end they do not satisfy our thirst.

Recently I read as a theme of a lecture: "Fulfilled desires are not fulfilling my desires." How true.

Our camping trip last summer led us to the French coast of the Mediterranean Sea—Cannes, Nizza, Monte Carlo. Thousands lay in the sun on the beach, like jumping fish taken out of the water. All year long these people had worked hard in order to afford these days at the ocean. However, the ocean is not the water of life for which they thirst without knowing it. The fulfilled desire of having these days at the ocean does not fulfill the deepest desires.

They comfort each other like somebody who wears glasses without any lenses and says, "Better than nothing!"

Coming without Thirst

The opposite is also possible: to come to the water but without thirst.

Like a medical treatment prescribed by a physician, the water of life is taken. Regular church attendance, Bible studies, even the daily reading of the Scriptures is carried out like a sacred duty. But there is no thirst.

A Japanese student who had lived at an Evangelical Youth Center for one year said to the pastor in charge, "The people who come here don't really desire all this." He had looked deep inside and had seen that they came but had no thirst.

Refusing to Accept

There is still a third possibility: to be thirsty, to come to the water of life, and yet stubbornly to refuse to accept it because it is free.

"Ho! Everyone who thirsts, come to the waters; and he who has no money, come, buy and eat! Come, buy wine and milk without money and without price" (Is 55:1).

Anything but this. To get it free is not what we want either. We are too proud for that. We think all kinds of spiritual chin-ups are necessary. At least the act of drinking has to be a little strenuous; otherwise, how could it satisfy thirst? We think that which costs nothing is worth nothing and therefore cannot help us.

If we do not take the water of life "without price," no one will get it at all, for the spring will dry up.

When the Spring Is Dried Up

The greatest challenge of our time: The thirsty do come. They want to take and drink. But the spring is dried up.

We truly live in a time of spiritual dryness. Many are still empty and thirsty when they come out of church. How is that possible? It is not the form of the service that matters but the content. Often the one who passes on the water of life is himself not thirsty anymore. The results of this are dried up little essays about God, full of harmless and correct statements but without any infectious and contagious virus, sterilized and chemically clean from every personal experience with God. Talks are no more helpful than sermons. The emptiness remains.

However, the water of life is still there, even today. For our time, too, the spiritual law of God's kingdom is still valid: Where the gospel is, congregations are formed. Where the water of life is offered, the thirsty come in great numbers, even today. No effort is too great. No trip is too far. When thirsty people come to the spring and drink, new life opens up. Only those who are thirsty can be satisfied.

Drinking in Vain

Now we have reached the last possibility of how to avoid the blessing which is offered in our verse. Another meaning of the phrase "for nothing, without price" is that all was in vain.

It is possible for someone to be thirsty and to come and drink the water of life, but "for nothing," "in vain." He drinks in vain because he does not pass it on.

"For to him who has will more be given, and he will have abundance; but from him who has not, even what he has will be taken away" (Mt 13:12). This is certainly one of the reasons for the dryness of our time for which we are all guilty. Is this why there are so many depressed Christians who spin their wheels, who turn around on their own axes?

God's Simple Offer

God's unconditional and whole offer is still valid today. It is the only offer in this world without a catch, being as simple as this: "If you are thirsty, come. If you want it, take the water of life—it costs nothing."

10

United States 1967: The Salt of the Earth

OUR LAST VACATION OUTING, on a beautiful late summer day, took us to the salt mine at Hallstatt in Austria. Salt was discovered there over 3,000 years ago.

More than twenty-eight miles of tunnels have been dug into the mountain. We had to slide part of the way on wooden chutes as we descended into the mountain. In the process we learned that a lot of diligence, effort, and not a little patience are necessary to get at the salt at all. It takes great intelligence and inventiveness to get it out and to bring it to a place where it can be used. More than 45,000 pounds are mined every hour.

That much? We were amazed at everything salt is used for. Salt is vital. People cannot live without salt. Life spoils without salt.

That is what Jesus means when he tells us, "You are the salt of the earth" (Mt 5:13). Each of us is a grain of salt! The followers of Jesus are as indispensible for the earth as salt is for food and the preservation of life.

But salt also has harmful effects; things can be oversalted. In the wrong place, the use of salt can even prove fatal. Some years ago in a maternity ward, salt was accidentally put in a sugar container and was put into the milk for one week before anyone noticed it. This caused eighteen infants to die.

Finally, salt can remain without effectiveness; it can become tasteless, as Jesus says. It is true that salt can never become unsalty—that is physically impossible—but it can be robbed of its strength. That happens either when it is not used at all (isolation from the world) or when it is mixed with other things in the wrong proportions and loses its power (assimilation into the world).

The questions arise at this latter point. Salt must be dissolved. But how can a grain of salt dissolve and still be salt? How can we share our saltiness and yet retain it? How can I identify myself with the world in order to reach it without being "conformed" to it (Rom 12:2)?

I was reminded of this tension in our Christian lives during my recent trip to America. The flight took only eight hours. The earth that we must salt is getting smaller. It takes just as long to drive from Lichtenberg, our home in Austria, to Mannheim, Germany, as it does to fly from Frankfurt to New York.

I had been invited by the American Lutheran Church to speak at two youth conferences. They were being held simultaneously in Seattle, Washington, and in Dallas, Texas, nearly 2,000 miles away. The speakers were flown between the two cities. Fifteen thousand young people between the ages of sixteen and eighteen had registered.

They were all staying in hotels. Bible studies were held in the mornings on the closed TV circuits of the hotel rooms. The participants were in groups of eight and had an older leader with whom they discussed the material after the broadcast. It was an interesting attempt to use mass communication so that even in a gathering of thousands the individual was taken into account and his or her needs were addressed.

The plenary session was held in the Colosseum which had been built in 1962 for the Seattle World's Fair and which seated 14,000. Everything was very modern. The message of being set free from selfishness through Christ was presented and performed by Wartburg College students in the form of a jazz musical. Otherwise, rock music was prevalent, even in the hymns during the worship services. Dr. Schoitz, president of the Lutheran World Federation, stood in the ecumenical worship service in his High Church robes next to a pair of guitar-strumming teenagers.

The conference was a bold attempt to reach the teenagers on their home ground and, as Paul became a

"Jew to the Jews" (1 Cor 9:20), to become a rock fan to the rock fans.

Salt in the form of rock music, or rock music in the form of salt? That is the question.

On the one hand: Does salt necessarily lose its savor when it is presented in the form of rock music? Why should a pipe organ be a better salt shaker than a guitar?

On the other hand: Is the rock music only used as salt to make a bland message palatable? Might the music accidentally become like frosting that takes the saltiness and bite out of the message and causes the loss of savor after all?

When the rock music had faded, it was my turn. A spotlight shone in my face, and I stood very much alone on the giant podium under blinding light. Everything around me sank into deepest night. Throughout the talk I felt as if I were swimming under water with no contact whatsoever with the audience, and every word I had written at my desk back home thundered ponderously back to me from a hundred loudspeakers. An infernal experience.

I had already lost all courage when I listened to the speakers who preceded me. Their talks were true works of art, adorned with anecdotes and inimitable humor. They punctuated their presentations by interruptions of recordings, and they used animated films to illustrate points.

I, on the other hand, had neither recordings nor films for support. I had nothing but a manuscript that Ingrid had lovingly corrected for me and that I read word for word. Against the background of the audiovisual wonderland that surrounded me, my presentation seemed so old-fashioned and out of place that some may have thought it was the latest method of mass communication.

But the contents of my talk were also far from modern. It was nothing but an exposition of Genesis 2:24 in the light of verse 25: only to those who have left their father and mother and who cleave to each other, being legally and publicly married, is given the promise of standing naked before each other without being ashamed and of becoming one.

During this message, so unmodern in form and content, a breathless silence prevailed. When I surfaced from my submarine voyage, I looked around in bewilderment and saw the supermodern American teenagers spontaneously standing up and clapping. It was as if I had proclaimed something completely new and unheard of. They applauded me almost as long as they had applauded the jazz musical. The conversations in my hotel room, conversations that lasted deep into the night, showed that my message had struck home.

The word is more powerful than pictures and sound. Only through the word is it promised that salt will spread. As long as we have this old and yet ever modern word with us, we will be grains of salt, able to go into the world with confidence. The word is the salt whose strength never decreases but increases more and more as we pass it on.

11

Acceptance and Love

I F THE FOLLOWING BIBLE VERSE SAID: "Love one another," we would not even feel challenged as we listen to it. It says, however: "Accept one another as Christ accepted us, to the glory of God" (Rom 15:7; NEB). The Amplified Bible says: "Welcome and receive . . . one another, then, even as Christ has welcomed and received you, for the glory of God."

If someone visits us, we take him in not only with his loveable traits or his sympathetic aspects, but we have to accept him as he is, including his weaker points and the little things that might even get on our nerves.

In our day, the word "love" has often been replaced by the word "acceptance." This is good. Romantic, sentimental, and also sexual misunderstandings of the word "love" are avoided. To love means first of all to accept the other one just as he is.

Why is this so difficult at the place of work, in the neighborhood, in family and marriage? The most common answer is: Because we love ourselves too much and because we only think about ourselves and only let ourselves count for something. This is why we cannot accept or love others. I would like to say just the opposite: Because we love ourselves too little, because we have not fully accepted ourselves. That is why it is so hard for us to accept others, to really love them.

The German psychotherapist Guido Groeger says, "It

is up to the theologian to decide how to interpret the word of the Lord, 'Love your neighbor as yourself'— whether as a commandment and a statement or as a double commandment. In any case, the psychologist has to underline the fact that there is in man no in-born self-love. Self-love is either acquired or it is non-existent. The one who does not acquire it or who acquires it insufficiently either is not able to love others at all or is able to love them only insufficiently. The same would be true for such a person also in his relationship to God."

If, on the one hand, self-acceptance is the foundation of our existence and, on the other hand, nobody is born with the ability to love and accept oneself, we face a real challenge. A tremendous task lies before us and we must ask ourselves:

Have I accepted myself fully and completely?

With my gifts? With my limits? With my dangers?

Have I accepted my place in life? My gender? My sexuality? My age?

Do I say yes to my marriage? To my children? To my parents? To my being single?

Do I say yes to my financial situation? To my state of health? To the way I look?

In short, do I love myself?

Dr. Paul Tournier tells about one of his patients who covered up all the mirrors whenever she entered a hotel room. She could not stand to see herself, especially when she was undressed. She had not yet accepted her body.

Only the one who has accepted himself can also accept others. "Love your neighbor as yourself" (Lv 19:18). Self-love is necessary before we can be freed from ourselves, and it is the requirement for our relationships with our fellow human beings.

How can we gain this—how can we learn to accept ourselves, to love ourselves? There is only one answer to this question; we must learn to let ourselves be loved. It is not enough that love is offered to us; we must also learn to receive it. We must learn to accept acceptance.

But what if we have never been accepted? What if our deficit of love has never been replenished? For many of us, the only answer seems to be to run away into addictions and drugs. But, we remain hopelessly alone. The vicious circle goes on and on; we do not love because we are not loved. We are not loved because we do not love.

Psychology can explain and describe this vicious circle, but it does not help us to escape. The circle cannot be broken from the inside. There must be an outside source: "Accept one another as Christ accepted us, to the glory of God."

Jesus Christ is the power from the outside breaking the vicious circle. He puts ground under our feet. He is the only one who accepts us as we are, fully, unconditionally, with all our wrappings.

Christ says: "Him who comes to me I will not cast out" (Jn 6:37). But when he accepts us, we cannot remain as we are. Acceptance is nothing but the first step of love. Luther stated in his fourth thesis which he nailed on the church door in Wittenberg, "God's love does not love that which is worthy of being loved, but it creates that which is worthy of being loved."

God's love is more than mere acceptance. It works and forms; it carves out the image which God has intended. Acceptance is the first step of love. But love is more—so much more—than acceptance.

My Journey Homeward · 50

12

Ethiopia 1967: Standing

"THEN IT WILL COME ABOUT IN THAT DAY that the nations will resort to the root of Jesse, who will stand as a signal for the peoples . . ." (Is 11:10).

A sign in the battle that stands unshakable in the midst of despair and helplessness, visible from afar as a signal flag on a mountain—that is our Lord Jesus Christ.

He stood on a mountain and shouted his message into the world.

Where people were suffering and dying, he stood and spoke his all-powerful and comforting message in the face of sickness and death.

He stood before those seeking direction and answered patiently and to the point, always trying to win the questioner.

He stood silently before Pilate and did not defend himself.

And then he stood again on the shore, when the disciples wanted to give up and start over as if he had never lived.

Even today, he is the only one who is really standing with us in our confused world as well as in our personal loneliness and helplessness, like that which I experience in an almost physical way before every new task.

It seems to me that a shimmer of his standing is reflected in us when he places us somewhere. To stand helplessly, only through him—that is the life of his witnesses.

Standing.

What Would You Have Answered?

When I arrived at Addis Ababa after a twelve-hour flight, an employee of Ethiopian Airlines approached me and asked to speak to me. She had written me a year before after reading one of my books. The friend who came to pick me up, Pastor Ezra Gebremedhin, remarked matter-of-factly, "You started as a counselor ten minutes after your arrival."

Ezra Gebremedhin is the pastor of the largest Protestant congregation in the central part of Addis Ababa. Every week he speaks on Radio Voice of the Gospel. Nowhere could we stop, get out of the car, go into a shop, or even walk ten steps without having someone speak to him. And he always let himself be detained and stood there with endless patience and friendliness.

It was a blessing that Ezra took the time to be my interpreter from English into Amharic at the pastors' conference. From the beginning, this ministry was a "standing" as a team of two. Rarely have I felt the support so deeply and joyously of being "alone together" in the act of proclaiming.

The pastors' conference meant that for three weeks we had to stand in a classroom and teach four seminars each day. Thirty pastors attended. Some had traveled more than 600 miles. Most of them were fathers of large families, lonely men from distant congregations in the bush where they had to travel by foot visiting the twenty or thirty villages entrusted to them. They were very grateful listeners.

One of my courses was a practical guide to counseling through word and deed. African churches—are they the only ones?—have a great vacuum in this area. Often the conversation had to be continued in the evening in my room. It was not always easy to step into the world of these pastors, to stand there and to stand up under their questions. For example: "When a heathen sends a goat into the desert as an offering to appease the gods, and a pastor catches it and eats it, and his congregation rejects him because of that—what can be done to reconcile the pastor and his congregation?"

What would you have answered?

Can Sex Hurt Love?

Soon it became clear that the message on marriage went beyond the scope of the pastors' conference. A professor of sociology at the University of Addis Ababa invited me to speak. I had announced the topic as: "Are Women Inferior to Men?" The lecture hall had 150 seats and was completely filled. I looked into extremely critical faces as I spoke, but they listened attentively. There were so many questions afterwards that I had to agree to hold another talk titled "Love."

The talk was supposed to take place in the meeting hall of a student dormitory where there was room for 300 people. An hour before the talk was to begin, the dormitory supervisor called to say the room was already filled. Soon there were students overflowing onto the street. We had to move to the nearest church.

Sitting in front of me, shoulder to shoulder, they filled every seat. There must have been five or six hundred people. Again I had to stand and face those expectant eyes. I experimented and delivered word for word the same talk I had presented to the youth of the United States in Seattle and Dallas.

It had the same effect. The only difference was that the

Africans did not stand up and applaud like the Americans but remained sitting, silent and deeply moved. Then hundreds of them raised their hands to ask questions. I had to ask that the questions be written on slips of paper, and I agreed to hold a third talk: "Can Sex Hurt Love?"

We looked for a room that would be large enough to hold the expected crowd. We were finally given permission to use the room that had been the reception hall for the Emperor of Ethiopia: Ras Makkonen Hall. It had more than a thousand seats.

No Standing Without Risk

My talk was planned for Saturday evening. I will never forget that day. It was a day when everything seemed to stagger; the only way to win the "rest" mentioned in the verse of the day, "So then, there remains a Sabbath rest for the people of God" (Heb 4:9), was to follow one step at a time, leaning on the "sign that stands."

Ingrid had left Lichtenberg on the morning of that day to join me in Addis Ababa. It was the first time she was able to be with me on a teaching trip to Africa. Friends had given the money for her travel expenses and were also caring for our children. So we decided to take the risk.

Would it all work out? Suddenly I had the feeling as if everything was at stake: marriage, children, family, the whole established work.

There is no standing without risk.

Then Ezra came with the news that the chairs had been removed from Ras Makkonen Hall and taken to the imperial palace for the state visit of President Jomo Kenyatta of Kenya. Only 175 chairs remained.

Nothing was certain. Should we cancel?

As Ezra worked feverishly to try to get chairs together

with two hours to go, I sat in his study preparing my talk, and Ingrid was boarding the plane in Frankfurt.

When I entered Ras Makkonen Hall at 7 P.M., I found myself in a majestic hall surrounded by columns. One-third of the space was filled with chairs. Behind the chairs stood walls of students. The aisles were packed. A group of girls sat anxiously on the floor in front of a column. I struggled slowly forward, climbing over heads and legs. There on the podium stood a last lonely empty chair for me. I didn't use it but instead sat demonstratively on the floor. At least those standing in the aisles followed my example. Their laughter told me I had established contact with them. Then it became quiet.

With my nerves on edge, I proceeded to hold what I believed to be my longest talk ever. I spoke for nearly two hours and tried to address each of the fifty-two groups of questions which they had written out for me the week before. Almost no one left the hall, not even those who had remained standing. When I was finished, Ezra had to run interference for me so I could leave the hall. I went to bed more than exhausted.

The next morning I was to preach in the Mekane-Yesus Church. At the same moment I stepped up to the pulpit, the door opened and Ingrid entered the church with Ezra's wife Gennet. She gave a personal testimony that was a seamless complement to my sermon. Not until after the service did we have a chance to greet one another.

Standing as a married couple is much more than standing as two individuals. During the following days of ministry together, we experienced over and over again that the most effective way the message about marriage can be presented is by a husband and wife together. To use Ezra's words: "The gift that was given for Ingrid's travel expenses bore fruit a hundredfold."

Part Two

A Walk through the Cultures

1

Marriage—The Same Message in All Five Continents

T HE MOST STRIKING EXPERIENCE is perceiving that the one message given to the Melanesians and the Germans, the Indonesians and the Austrians, the Ethiopians, Camerounians and the Americans, affected them all in exactly the same way.

How is that possible? The answer is in Deuteronomy 9:3: "Know therefore this day that he who goes over before you . . . is the Lord your God . . ."

A Bible verse written nearly 3,000 years ago (Gn 2:24) can help people living in all continents today. Our lectures were basically only interpretations of this one verse.

This is the only verse about marriage that is cited four times in the Bible—Genesis 2:24; Matthew 19:5; Mark 10:7; Ephesians 5:31—"Therefore a man leaves his father and his mother, and cleaves to his wife, and they shall become one flesh."

This simple sentence states the three elements essential to marriage.

The word "leaving" indicates that a public and legal act has taken place. Sometimes in Africa the whole wedding party dances, often for many miles, from the village of the bride to the village of the bridegroom. There is nothing secret about it. From that day on everyone knows that these two are husband and wife; they are under "wedlock."

In our day, this legal act of leaving is replaced by a public announcement before the wedding, as well as by an official marriage license. What is important is that a public and legal action takes place.

The word "cleaving" means love, but love of a special kind. It is love which has made a decision and which is no longer a groping and seeking love. Love which cleaves is mature love, love which has decided to remain faithful—faithful to one person—and to share with this one person one's whole life.

The words "one flesh" describe the physical aspect of marriage. This physical aspect is as essential for marriage as the legal and personal aspect. The physical union between husband and wife is as much within God's will for marriage as is leaving the parents and cleaving to each other.

Spelled out, this message means that if you separate one element of marriage from the two others, everything falls apart. If there is no love, no cleaving, then we have the "empty marriage." This emptiness causes suffering in the physical aspect, and when that is not in order, we have the "hungry marriage." This often leads to the temptation of infidelity. If there is no legal marriage—we call that the "stolen marriage"—then sex and love are in tension with each other and both lose their meaning. Almost all marriage sickness can be diagnosed in these three groups.

Young people who are preparing for marriage now must make their goal the uniting of all three elements. They can then see which premarital behavior leads to the goal and which does not. Those who do not succeed pass by real marriage.

This message is so simple that sometimes we were ashamed to proclaim it in the light of all the complicated books written about this theme. We are thankful to the Africans who taught us to speak with biblical simplicity and imagery so that now even the West understands us.

The missionary message of marriage in Christ includes also singles in its dynamic of leaving, cleaving, and becoming one flesh. Paul says, "This mystery is great."

Once after a seminar in Europe, a young Frenchman said to me, "Am I not right, the whole subject of marriage is for you just an excuse to evangelize?"

I answered: "For me, marriage is the best landing strip for the gospel in our times."

Maybe the urgent needs of marriages worldwide in our day are but a form of God's presence going before us in order to prepare this landing strip.

Even when we are far away from him, God is near to us. This is the heart of the gospel. Even in the midst of the dying world of those who are far away from God, we experienced what a wonderful thing it is to have the privilege of testifying to the nearness of the God of life. Slowly we understood that this is the goal and target of our message about marriage and family.

2

Australia 1976:
The West Has Lost the Will to Live

A S WE LEFT HOME WE WONDERED why we had been invited to Australia of all places. Would the long trip be worth our time and all the expenses? In the course of our counseling and lecturing during those weeks, we found out why we had come.

As far as being on its way to death, Australia is just a few steps ahead of Europe. This began perhaps with the use of the contraceptive pill. For the first time in history, medicine tried to prevent life. The next step on the course of anti-life is sterilization. More and more couples marry with the declared intention never to have children, and even student couples have themselves sterilized before marriage if they marry at all.

Linked with this hostility to children and life is the use of abortion—the next step on the course to death. Once you begin to touch the process of preventing life, there is no end to it. The practice of euthanasia for infants having birth defects (or who are unwanted?) and the conscious decision to end the lives of the old and sick is a logical consequence. In Australia there is even a demand for a law to be passed that legalizes "assisted suicide."

Marriage, too, is caught up in this run of death. A new law in Australia, "The Family Law Act," enables couples to draw up marriage contracts valid for only one year. The new slogan is "creative divorce." Divorce is no longer considered an unfortunate event but an ideal situation, a desirable goal. Since this law went into effect, the divorce rate has risen 140 percent.

All this eventually reaches us, too. The only difference is that in Australia the signs are already visible while here they still remain unseen. Everybody who is ready to make a compromise concerning the issue of sterilization and abortion, even the consumption of the pill, has to be aware that they have given in to the anti-life course, the consequences of which no one can foresee.

The poet and prophet Solzhenitsyn made a true observation with his words: "The West has lost the will to live." The West has lost its will to live because they have lost God. If it is true that Jesus Christ is life, then where he is absent, death rules. We live in a death-oriented world. Theoretically and theologically we always knew that. Now it becomes reality. Death becomes in its truest meaning "the reward of sin," the inescapable consequence of being far away from God.

3

Tensions

MY TRIP TO THE UNITED STATES began in Berlin. The topic I had chosen for my lecture purposely avoided relevant problems of today: "Marriage Counseling—An Open Door for Missions." When I looked at the printed invitation sheet, I realized that the directors in charge of the conference had nicely rearranged and updated my topic to: "Marriage Counseling—Help for Society."

At this occasion I asked myself just how many tensions I would have to deal with at the same time: the tension between the vertical dimension (our relationship to God) and the horizontal dimension (our relationship to others); between giving advice and spiritual counseling; between traditional ethics and new morality; between narrow-minded, mission field philosophy and ecumenical broadness; between the extremely pious Christians for whom the topics of marriage and love are not sacred enough and the atheists who find it not objective enough to argue from the standpoint of faith. Underlying it all is the tension which I must endure as a creative person who constantly fights against the deadly attacks of institutions and yet who needs their support.

When I became aware of this I felt the desire to be myself in quietness and not to talk or write anymore. If the monthly text would not have read, "All things are possible to him who believes" (Mk 9:23), I would have been tempted to get off the plane which carried me unrelentingly to the United States.

4

Everything Goes Its Own Way

A GOOD FRIEND TOLD US that he has used this sentence in one of his sermons. By changing the pronoun from "its" to "his," it becomes a positive, resurrection message: "Everything goes his way."

Certainly there were many people who stood and gazed at the cross where Jesus hung, thinking with resignation, "There you have it again! If somebody wants to do something good and bring healing power into this world, they destroy him. Everything does go its own way."

The angel of the Lord, however, changed all this. He rolled away the stone and sitting on it, he proclaimed, "The Crucified One is risen." Out of death came life, out of despair came hope, out of the end came the beginning. Everything goes his way—always downward into the depths before it can go upward into heaven.

Today God goes his way, yes, even through the extreme confusion which reigns in the field of marriage. There is a great division which becomes more abysmal the closer we approach the end time. Because this world goes its own way, God goes his way through this world.

What impressed us during personal talks at the time of our last trip to the United States was the consequences that took place in the lives of those who had made a decision for Christ. If you ask a student in the United States how long he has been a Christian, you get a clear answer. From that moment on, he draws the consequences for his sexual behavior. The faith of a person is often revealed through this change in behavior. Only with a background of darkness can light truly shine. Behaviorisms which were considered normal and a matter of course in earlier times, like getting a marriage license before living together, all of a sudden have testimonial character. Christians and non-Christians are clearly separated here. Everything goes his way.

5

Life's Limits

THE DISCUSSION ABOUT ABORTION brings up this question: when does life begin, and from which moment on is killing really killing? When we believe—and this is our fixed conviction—that human life begins with a wonderful fusion of egg and sperm, then its beginning is a mystery.

One could even go further in looking to Jeremiah 1:5: "Before I formed you in the womb I knew you." Is not our own life, our spiritual life, our life in God which will carry us beyond death, determined much earlier in an incomprehensible mystery of God? What a responsibility to touch life!

The limits of the end of life have become hazy, too, now that it is possible to transplant organs. From which moment on is a person dead enough to justify the transplantation of organs? Is a person ever "dead," since the death barrier was broken through at Easter? Since Christ broke into the spiritual origin of our real lives? "Before I formed you in the womb I knew you" (Jer 1:5).

6

Revolt of the Couples

A S THE MISERY IN MARRIAGES INCREASES worldwide and divorce rates rise, the institution of marriage is attacked and proclaimed guilty. Marriage has been proclaimed dead, old-fashioned, dangerous for one's health, destructive to love; it has been ridiculed and scoffed at in films, and described as boring, dull, a prison whose bars and walls need to be broken down.

Experiments are made with new forms of marriage: trial marriages, triangle marriages, group marriages, and every form of polygamy—more than one wife at the same time or one after the other—yet the suffering and distress of marriages has not been alleviated.

Then the researchers came. With scientific objectivity, they stated exactly and objectively what was happening in the marriages. When they were asked, however, what should happen in marriages, they had no answer.

Then educators took over, held lectures, and diligently passed on information. As important as that was and is, the behavior of the marriage partners didn't change.

Finally, the clinicians appeared, professional counselors, among them the psychologists, physicians, theologians, and lawyers. They doctored the sick and dying marriages. Even though they had success now and then, they made one essential mistake; they had no preventive measures for those marriages which were not yet sick.

No one seemed to care about those marriages which

were still healthy but whose growth was somehow stagnated. Attention was given only to those marriages which had sunk into a problematic state and were needing clinical care. Cynics and skeptics were given evidence anew that the institution of marriage had failed as such.

Now after all the attempts have failed, something new is happening in the world today. Basically this is the most obvious, logical, and simple consequence; the couples arise and defend marriage. They come out of their holes. They organize themselves and stand up in front of the enemy, not in that they give arguments but in that they demonstrate a good and healthy marriage. They work on marriage beginning with their own.

There are two reasons why nobody had thought of something so simple and sanctifying. First, marriage was considered to be something which would function on its own with everyone doing what is right by instinct, as if no education and preparation would be necessary. Consequently, everyone who could not get along without external help was looked upon as incapable and stupid.

Second, marriage was thought of as very private, and under no circumstances should this privacy be exposed to another couple. Through this exaggeration and over-emphasizing of the intimacy of marriage, couples passed up the help they could have given to each other.

7

Papua, New Guinea 1975:
"... and Sit with Him"

WHEN PHILIP STOPPED THE CHARIOT of the Secretary of the Treasury of the Ethiopian queen on the road to Gaza, he was invited by the Secretary "to come up and sit with him." Philip accepted and thus placed himself on the same level as his counselee. He won the first African for Christ.

We were reminded of this story in Acts 8 when we were invited to New Guinea, the largest island of the earth, to conduct six marriage seminars there. Since the participants were to come only as couples, many had to bring their babies along. It was awkward for a mother to handle her baby while sitting on a chair, so Pastor Janadabing Apo, our interpreter, had the splendid idea that all of us would simply sit on the floor.

This proved to be an excellent way of establishing contact. A relaxed, informal atmosphere, combined with the feeling of belonging together, was the result. Confidence was established without effort, and we experienced the importance of "sitting with him."

Imagine fifteen couples sitting on mats on the floor of an uncluttered room. The babies slept, having been nursed or gently rocked in the strong net bags which the mothers carried on their foreheads. The bishop and his wife, the district president, nurses, teachers, pastors, and theological students were among the participants, as well as simple villagers and fishermen.

Besides the deepening of the spiritual life of husband and wife and teaching about all aspects of marriage, one of the major goals in our seminars was to practice communication. The first day each husband had to shake hands with his wife. Some were unable to do it, so they practiced in their rooms all by themselves. The next day they could do it with more ease. Then we practiced looking at each other. First the men among themselves, then the women, and finally each couple.

The third day we practiced talking. Each one had to think of three things he especially liked about his partner. After a time of quiet reflection, the couples went outside one by one and sat down together. Facing each other, each husband had to tell his wife and each wife her husband these three things in their mother tongue. Some needed more than an hour before they finished.

The following day the couples could volunteer to share with a group what they had told each other. To our surprise, they were very willing to do this. A sense of reliability seemed to be what they most appreciated. In such a time of change—New Guinea became independent in September, 1975—there seemed to be an overwhelming need to have someone upon whom one could depend.

We shall never forget a young teacher who reminded us of an Assyrian warrior, with his dark eyes, aquiline nose, and magnificent black beard. He sat down with his wife in the center of the group circle and said to her, "I love you because you do not want me to die, for you give me to eat." Then he could not hold back his tears of joy that he had been able to verbalize his feelings. It is strange, but evidently the feeling of being loved can only enter through the ear.

During the first three seminars in Madang, Finschhafen, and Malolo, Ingrid could not yet be with us, so our oldest son Daniel had to replace his mother. He explained in his quiet and clear manner, with the help of slides, the process of fertilization, pregnancy, and birth. He also showed Dr. Vellay's film of five births where the father is part of the birth team.

The fact that all this teaching came from Daniel made a deep impression on the New Guineans. They couldn't get over the fact that a young, unmarried man was allowed to know and to talk about all these "secrets"—all this in the presence of his father! Daniel's lecture said more about family life education than a long lecture on our part would have done.

The last seminar in New Guinea was for missionary couples; six American, three Australian, one Canadian, and one German couple participated. We didn't have to change our topics of discussion. Their problems were very similar to those of the New Guineans: communication and dealing with fertility. But the missionaries had a special need for someone "to sit with them" and listen.

8

We Walked in the Dark; Now We Have Seen the Light

THE HIGHLIGHT OF MY LIBERIAN TRIP in 1968 was a conference with evangelists. This took place in a far off bush village named Zorzor near the border of Guinea. The evangelists in this case were lay preachers who were in charge of services and devotions in their own villages. One pastor often served more than thirty villages.

Once a month the evangelists gathered together in Zorzor, a centrally located village, for prayer meetings, Bible studies, and spiritual fellowship. I had asked the missionary in charge to invite the women to my lectures and to have someone to help with the small children.

Each lecture seemed to open up a new world to these people. One of them said at the end of our meetings: "We walked in the dark; now we have seen the light."

I was filled with deep joy—a joy that can only be felt when you do the work God gives you and stand at the place God puts you. All that was missing in Zorzor was my Ingrid and the standing together as a couple in the place God has put us. If Ingrid could have been there, and maybe even our African co-workers, Jean and Ernestine Banyolak, then it would have been perfect. An effective course on marriage has to be taught by couples for couples.

Will there be ears to hear and eyes to see that here a door is opened through which the God of glory wants to move into Africa?

Tchollire 1969

On a six-week lecture trip through the area of Rey Bouba in northern Cameroun, my co-worker, Jean Banyolak, and I drove through the jungle and the savanna, slept in twenty-three beds, held thirty-two lectures and five services together, and each day we became more of a team. Being a guest of our African co-worker was a new experience for me on this trip. After going through customs in Douala, I passed through a heavily guarded door and was embraced openly by an African man and his wife. We then traveled to their own home in a taxi which they paid for: what a difference from our first arrival in Cameroun sixteen years ago!

Later we were picked up by missionaries, and we lived at the mission station that resembled somehow an unapproachable fortress from which we would make expeditions into the unknown African land. Now I was a guest in an African home, and I counted it a great privilege. To be a guest makes the advent of Jesus Christ visible: "Sing and rejoice . . . for lo, I come and I will dwell in the midst of you" (Zec 2:10).

God became a guest. He did not build a fortress from which he conquered the world. He came to the world as a guest—long and passionately awaited but still surprising his hosts. He won over those who cared for him. He required also that his disciples become guests.

The guest surrenders to his host like a child in the crib. He does not demand. He allows everything that is done to him to happen. Because he is poor and dependent on his host, everything the guest brings with him is taken in more willingly. At the end of the visit, the gift which the guest gives to his host will be received like the guest himself was.

The longer we traveled together the more Jean took the role as the leader and I the role of the accompanying guest. This opened many doors. Jean made the first contacts, organized, and planned our lecture themes. Because of this, my message appeared in a way that was not thought of as merely European. Jean made credible the idea that the modern Western image of marriage stands much further away from the biblical image than the heathen image of the original African tradition.

The further we went north, the more often I had to interpret Jean's French into Fulani and use this language myself. Even though I had not spoken one word of Fulani for twelve years, this language slowly awakened—like Africans say—from sleep. Since I had not expected this, it was a special gift for me.

This happened in Tchollire, the last leg of our trip! The seeds Ingrid and I had sown there together sixteen years ago had grown. The church had 800 baptized members, was financially independent, and supported seventy preaching stations that were cared for by ten catechists.

Before I left, I gave a party. Two hundred guests attended from Tchollire and the surrounding area. Rice with beef was served in big washtubs. For dessert we had candied peanuts. Then the overwhelming joy had to be expressed in that most spontaneous expression of the African soul: dance. Suddenly drums and hand-held clicking pieces of wood appeared. A huge circle was formed and we all sang and danced—Jean and I, too—for two hours around the circle in the moonlight: the missionary was a guest.

Poli 1971

At a marriage seminar in Poli, North Cameroun, we were up against considerable opposition. When we said that to become "one flesh," a couple must also share their money and personal property, some of the participants were so upset we thought the whole seminar might break up. Man and woman had strictly separate goods. Not only did each have his own money but each also had his field, his cattle, his storage shed. If a spouse were to die, the family-in-law of the living would immediately take back their possessions. No wonder the message of Genesis 2:24, ". . . and they become one flesh," caused a small revolution.

In such situations it is necessary to have African co-workers. Jean and Ernestine Banyolak came from Douala with their two-year-old daughter Elizabeth. Together we worked as a team—a white couple and a black couple.

It was indescribable how Jean and Ernestine realistically acted out different situations in marriage under the theme "Acceptance and Love" so that everybody could easily understand. Jean handled the delicate theme of money with great calmness and objectivity. Everyone was able to accept the message, even though it was hard on them.

The greatest response came from Jean's lecture about "The Pair and the Parasites." At first we thought that he would target in on the family-in-law. But no, he really meant bugs, fleas, lice, flies, gnats, ants, mice, rats. As Europeans we would never have thought of using these pests for the subject of a lecture on marriage. Jean was right: they do bother the African family life considerably. People listened with fascination and gratefulness. Jean had a remedy for everything. Afterwards there was a run on the sack of mousetraps which Jean had brought with him. The women stood in line to let Ernestine use a disinfectant on their heads. They were not bashful, but felt accepted and loved.

We spent the last days before departure at the cozy home of the Banyolaks in Douala. It radiated order and cleanliness but most of all peace. We made plans and had the feeling that we had just begun our work now that we had grown together as a team. We also had enough literature and had gained a great deal of experience. At that moment we received a letter from our supporting group in Geneva. We were told that they could no longer provide financial assistance for our work because cuts in their budget were necessary.

In the Kingdom of God, service is the same as reward. "My reward is that I have the privilege of serving." That's why those workers in the vineyard who begin work in the last hour are really the deprived ones.

2

You Are a Good Word for Us
Indonesia and New Caledonia 1970

"HE WENT ON HIS WAY REJOICING" (Acts 8:39) was the watchword on January 10 as I got on the Boeing 707 in Frankfurt. The Indian stewardess, dressed in a sari, waited with hands folded in front of her breast and greeted each passenger with a deep bow. Precisely at 2:30 P.M. we took off. Shortly afterwards the pilot announced, "At your right is Munich, then we will fly over Salzburg, and in about twenty minutes we will be over Zagreb." Only an unending sea of clouds was visible, where here and there gray mountain tops peeked above the even white snow field. At 600 miles per hour we raced over the Alps.

At 6:15 P.M. we landed in Beirut. The following 2,600

miles to Bombay took us four hours and twenty-five minutes. I asked for a map in order to get myself oriented. We flew over Saudi Arabia, the Persian Gulf, and the Arabian Sea and were served hot rice, lamb, and vegetables. Later, we departed from Bombay, had two short layovers in Madras and Singapore, passed Sumatra, and landed in Djakarta, Indonesia.

I had one hour to rest before the first youth meeting.

The next day another meeting was scheduled with several hundred young men and women attending. They listened intently. The questions they asked afterwards were the same as in Germany, Austria, the United States, Ethiopia, South Africa, and Cameroun. It would seem that not only the airports are alike in this world.

Three days later, shortly before midnight, I was still continuing my journey to Sydney, Australia. I made my flight connection in the afternoon to Nouméa, the capital of New Caledonia, an island that lies about 1550 miles east of Australia. It was 7:00 P.M. when we landed. My watch, which I had not reset since my departure, showed 5:00 in the morning. That made it a ten hour time difference; it was easy to picture what our children were doing. When we were getting up, they were going to bed the night before.

Ingrid's airplane arrived the next morning. It had been two nights and a day since she left Paris.

Our 155-mile car trip to the college of Do-Neva took us through a constantly changing mountainous landscape. When Captain Cook, who first discovered the island in 1774, saw this landscape, he was reminded of Scotland. That is also why the island is called New Caledonia. Half of the 100,000 inhabitants are Europeans, mostly of French origin. The other half are natives who belong to the Melanesian race, one of the oldest races known to the world: dark brown skin, protruding cheekbones, thick lips, a broad nose, and brown eyes.

This is the way the people looked who attended our marriage seminar. We were introduced with a speech—"You Are a Good Word for Us!"—to which we had to respond formally. As usual, Ingrid did a better job than I did. Then they gave us a bouquet of flowers that was intertwined with a few currency bills: "C'est la coutume"—that's the custom!

It was January, which happened to be the hottest time of the year. The first days were strenuous until we slowed down from the European working pace and adjusted to the rhythm of life there.

One half of our group were native Melanesians who came from the three eastern islands of Maré, Lifu, and Uvéa. The other half were from New Caledonia itself, which is called "la grande terre," the big land, or the big earth. For the people there, the world consists of these three islands and "the big earth." The rest is water. It took a while for us to adjust to this view of the world.

A man who worked at a radio station and was also a YMCA secretary was the only Polynesian, from Tahiti. Among the others were six pastors, six male teachers, and one female teacher. All were married except four young girls and two young men, but only three men had brought their wives with them.

Imagine this: a seminar with twenty-two people for four weeks! Where else could people of such different origins live together in a confined place for that length of time, not only taking time for each other but also creating the message they want to carry on? It was an unbelievable opportunity but also an enormous responsibility. At the same time the strength of our own marriage was tested daily. The listeners could immediately feel whether we were just lecturing or if we were actually living our marriage.

We grew very close to the Melanesian people. A part of the closeness came as we shared their food: sago, sweet potatoes, cassava, green papaya vegetables which tasted just like sauerkraut, roasted shark with bamboo shoot salad, fruit salad with pineapple, bananas, mangoes, and coconut juice.

Everyone could speak French well enough so that we could teach in that language. Everything we said they soaked up like dry sponges.

Their problems were similar to those in Africa. While sociologists seem to be fascinated by the differences in the cultures, we are more fascinated by the similarities. For example, as in many African tribes, the Melanesians believe that the father's semen will poison the nursing mother's milk. This is the reason why parents do not sleep together for long periods of time after the birth of a child. The literature in French which we had written for use in Africa could be used here. It was touching to see their desire for the printed word.

We did not find any polygamy. That may be because the husband helps his wife in the field work. We had the impression that there was a greater friendship between the sexes than anywhere we had been. Melanesians are very sportsminded and are good athletes. Women and men played happily together at the evening volleyball games, something we seldom witnessed in Africa.

When Ingrid gave her lectures on the theme "Understanding Your Wife," she showed the women the relaxation techniques for pregnancy and birth. The men immediately wanted to join the women to learn these exercises. At once the whole group was lying on the floor relaxing.

Speaking about intimate personal problems often leads to the recognition of sin and a new experience of grace. That is why personal counseling was an integral part of the seminar. Gradually these talks became a time of confession and forgiveness with the vertical dimension —the relationship to God—replacing the horizontal.

When we looked back, we realized that we had held marriage seminars in five different continents during a six-month period. Humanly this was an impossibility— adjusting to so many different situations, cultures, and people in such a short time. Yet we had felt God's presence in our frailty: "Know therefore this day that he who goes over before you . . . is the Lord your God" (Dt 9:3).

In New Caledonia I became ill as never before in my life. At first the doctor thought it was malaria. Later it was diagnosed as a kidney infection. What a provision of God that Ingrid could be with me and take care of me.

On the last day before my trip back home, Samuel, one of the teachers, straightforwardly asked if he might give me a hug. He said he had learned how to love Christ, how to love his wife, and how to love his children at this seminar. Now he wanted not only to talk about Christ but to live Christ. He had never hugged a European before. This was his way of thanking me.

10

Sowing and Reaping

Finland 1974

"WELCOME TO THE END OF THE WORLD!" was the greeting that we received from the student delegation that picked us up at the airport in Helsinki. We both felt that way too, for we were fighting colds, and at the same time we had a sense of emptiness, the same feeling we got whenever we had to leave home to start another journey.

The letter that we had received prior to going to Finland had informed us of their country's most serious problems. Alcohol abuse is a very common problem among young people. The suicide rate is one of the highest in Europe. Most of the mothers are professional women and have no more than two children. Abortion is widespread. Mothers have to leave the hospital early after giving birth because their beds are needed for abortion patients.

The first thing we had to do was to hold a press conference. The next day, when it was too late, we thought of the best answers to the reporters' questions.

During our seminars, the students listened to us silently and patiently, showing almost no reaction. This did not help us in overcoming our feelings of insecurity. But slowly they warmed up, and now and then they even dared to laugh.

Afterwards, the students seemed to have unlimited time to ask questions and discuss our lectures, for the nights in Finland are very long. The daylight began at nine o'clock in the morning and already at three in the afternoon it grew dark. Supper was usually at five o'clock, and afterwards you had lots of time.

Right from the beginning there were some things we did not understand. The hostility against children seemed even greater than in Germany. It was almost a hatred of children. Parents who expected a third child were embarrassed and felt like outcasts, even though they wanted the child.

In their professional lives, we found women to be very self-confident and to have an unusual drive for independence while the men seemed more introverted and insecure. However, in their personal lives, we found apathy and self-hatred among young women as we had never witnessed before. Some of them could absolutely not believe that there was anything lovable about them.

We found a strange theology in Finland: if you really want to please God, you don't dare find anything good about yourself. If you want to be accepted by God, you mustn't accept yourself. Any positive statement about yourself could lead to pride which is unsuitable for Christians.

Out of this heresy comes a mood of religiosity which somehow matches the long nights and the cold, depressive Nordic landscapes very well.

Ethiopia 1969

On the night flight from Rome to Asmara, I slept so well that I didn't notice when supper was served. When I first looked out the plane window at dawn, I saw the gray-brown peaks of the mountains of northern Ethiopia. How different their loneliness is from that of the Alps. The mountain peaks in the Alps seem somehow to have an inviting shine, while to me the bare ridges of African mountains, on which the sun beats down mercilessly, have the appearance of complaining and suffering, of being almost repulsive.

Asmara, this small, clean, friendly city in Eritrea, was the site of the Missions Conference at which I was to give a report. In the discussions it became clear how concerned the African church leaders are that the western spirit of so-called "new morality" could gain a foothold in Africa. I saw once again how much I am caught between two fronts in my work. There are still churches in Africa that would rather not have their young people reading my book *I Loved a Girl* because it is too free and modern, while in Germany it is often rejected because it is too old-fashioned and conservative. Sometimes it isn't easy to let yourself be under fire from both sides and still maintain your position. But Jesus also stood between the fronts, and perhaps it is true here, too, that the disciple is not greater than his master.

In Addis Ababa, for the Radio Voice of the Gospel, I had ten radio programs to record that I had written about the family budget. During this process I learned how differently one must write when the material is for listeners rather than for readers. As an "actor" in the drama, I also learned how differently one must speak when the voice alone must carry the message without the help of facial expression or gesture.

At one time the recording technician said to me, "You

must smile when you speak. Then your voice will sound completely different." Should we smile when we write so that it will read differently? Or even think with a smile so that we will treat each other differently?

South Africa 1969: God's Angels and Civil Servants

The confusion of tongues at the Tower of Babel is no longer the greatest divider of peoples. Today we have much more effective distinctions: passports, visas, and immunization cards.

It is easy to get a tourist visa to travel in South Africa if you only want to visit those areas where the whites live. But if you, as we, wanted to get into contact with the nonwhites (ratio of white to nonwhite is 1:4) and to enter the so-called "Batustans" or "Homelands" where nonwhites are forced to live, then each district commissioner must grant special permission. For this reason the processing of the application for such a visa takes four months.

When I wanted to depart on my trip, my passport was still (after five months) at the South African consulate in Munich. Only because an understanding passport official issued a duplicate passport was I able to start my trip to Ethiopia at all. In this age of bureaucracy, angels sometimes must also take the form of civil servants.

So I waited in Addis Ababa for the passport with the South African visa. Exactly one hour before my flight to Johannesburg, it arrived by air mail. But even that would not have happened if a South African missionary had not made a courageous personal effort with the passport office. "I acted according to the example of the petitioning widow," he wrote from Pretoria.

Ingrid had similar difficulties. Since she wanted to visit Jean and Ernestine Banyolak in Douala on the way home and would have to spend the night in Brazzaville, she needed a transit visa for the Congo. But at the time the Congo did not have diplomatic relations with the United States, so not only was her transit visa refused but also her United States passport was simply held by the consulate of the Congo in Bonn. However, Ingrid also found an angel in the form of a civil servant who issued a duplicate passport for her. Otherwise, she would not have been able to travel even without the visa for South Africa. When the South African visa came, it was on a separate sheet. If it had been in her passport she might have had difficulties traveling to other African countries that have broken diplomatic relations with South Africa because of its racial policies. This is our world!

There was yet another complication for Ingrid. Her immunization card was in the passport that was being held at the consulate of the Congo. Fortunately—or more accurately, through the guidance of God, whose plan takes our mistakes into account—she had mislaid this immunization card once before and had had a duplicate issued, only to find the original again later. If it had not been for this circumstance, she would not have been able to go.

You can imagine we felt as if we were dreaming when we met at exactly the planned time—on May 12 at 12:15 P.M.—at the Jan Smuts airport in Johannesburg.

Three hours later we were speaking together for the first time in South Africa at a teachers' convention in one of the settlements for nonwhite workers outside Johannesburg. Ingrid was completely alert even though she had been on the plane all night. That evening the first public lecture was held in downtown Johannesburg, and on the following day there was a meeting with 140 African pastors.

The Five Functions of a Woman

The major task was still ahead of us: a week of talks at a theological school north of Durban. The churches had sent twenty married couples, primarily pastors and their wives. The professors and the students at the theological school were also participating in the talks.

We conducted five sessions a day, each one hour long. I had three and alternated with Ingrid who had two. It was a unique and joyous experience to work as a team in the sense of Genesis 2:18: "I will make him a helper fit for him." In retrospect, we can say that it would not have been possible to accomplish the task otherwise.

Our main mission in Africa was to replace the image of a woman as a "thing" or a "fruitful garden" with the contrasting image that expresses her humanity and individuality and the fact that she is made in the image of God, just as a man is. Only a woman can accomplish this mission, and then not so much through what she says as through what she is.

Ingrid said that while a man has only one function in reproduction, a woman is more complicated. She has five reproductive functions: ovulation, the act of love, pregnancy, childbirth, and breastfeeding. Never had the Africans heard a woman speaking of these things, and she was doing it in front of a mixed audience. Ingrid broke all the taboos. That she succeeded and her message was received thankfully is due to the work of the Spirit who was poured out upon us at Pentecost and who makes possible the impossible.

In an hour of thanksgiving at the end of the week, the Africans expressed the same idea over and over again; it became clear to them that the Christian faith and sexuality belong together. Indeed, only through faith could the area of sexuality be understood and mastered.

Rhodesia 1978: Whatever a Man Sows

The waters of the Zambezi fell without ceasing into the deep before us. Every minute over 132,000,000 gallons plunge into a chasm one mile wide and 300 feet deep, sending spray clouds spinning high into the sky. The constant roar of these greatest waterfalls in the world was to us a sign of God's never-ending and ever-renewing grace as we experienced them once again during this trip.

In order to have more time for writing, we tried to limit our African or Asian travel to one trip a year. This time we were led to accept an invitation to Rhodesia (now Zimbabwe) to teach at a Christian Leadership Conference for more than 500 pastors, teachers, and Christian leaders held at the University of Rhodesia in Salisbury. Later on we spent a few days at Victoria Falls, discovered by David Livingstone in 1855 and where Ingrid's father spent some time 35 years ago on his way from Capetown to Tanzania shortly before his death. The airport bus which took us from the airport to Victoria Falls was escorted by an armored car. On each side of the road danger signs warned us of mines. In our hotel room, explicit instructions told us what to do in case of an attack.

After our arrival in Salisbury (now Havare) on September 2, it did not take us long to realize that we were in the midst of a civil war. The city of Salisbury, certainly one of the most beautiful in the world, was bathed in warm spring sunshine under a clear blue sky, and its lilac jacaranda trees were in full bloom. But we saw the white Rhodesians who came from the countryside into the city get out of their cars with ammunition belts over their shoulders and machine guns in their hands. It was dangerous to travel from town to town except in a convoy. Daily the front pages of the newspapers reported war casualties. The public seemed hardened to it. It was estimated that sixty people died on both sides each day. The same number left the country, even though they had to sell their property at a loss and could not take their money with them. Outwardly everything seemed calm and normal in the city, but it was an eerie calm.

Spiritually it was healthy for us to be in danger. The words of Psalm 71 came to life: "In Thee, O Lord, do I take refuge. . . . In Thy righteousness deliver me and rescue me. . . . Be Thou to me a rock of refuge, [to which I may continually come]. . . . For Thou art my rock and my fortress."

After reading this psalm we heard the news that the opposition forces operating out of neighboring Zambia and Mozambique had downed a Rhodesian Airlines plane, on its regular flight between Kariba and Salisbury, by means of a heat-seeking missile from inside the country. This meant that air travel was no longer safe.

Great bitterness was caused by the fact that ten of the eighteen survivors of the crash, all suffering from shock after the forced landing in the wilderness, were brutally killed by blacks who appeared on the spot almost instantly with the accusation, "You have taken away our country!" Among those murdered were also women and children. One shudders to see what man is capable of when hatred that has grown for decades deep under the surface suddenly explodes.

Yet this cruel deed reflects the hard truth expressed in Galatians 6:7: "Do not be deceived, God is not mocked, for whatever a man sows, that he will also reap." The following verse adds: "For he who sows to his own flesh will from the flesh reap corruption," or as the Good News Bible says, "gather the harvest of death."

To sow to your own flesh means to pursue your own interest, fulfilling your own natural desires while closing your eyes to reality, and to keep on living as if nothing would ever change. The whites of Rhodesia, outnumbered fifteen to one by the blacks, had deliberately closed their eyes without seeing the handwriting on the wall. Few Africans had been trained for leadership either in the government or in the church. The government tried to establish majority rule by January 1, 1979, using the support of moderate black politicians. Many years ago when we witnessed the fight for independence in Cameroun, this would have been a revolutionary deed. It would have shown to the world that black and white could work together constructively. But in Rhodesia it seemed, humanly speaking, too late for such a solution, and the bitter "harvest of death" had to be reaped.

Having lived in Cameroun for twelve years, we were sensitized as to whether or not there was a bridge between the races or at least the beginning of mutual understanding. After our weeks spent in Rhodesia, our impression was that black and white were further apart there than in any other African country we had visited except South Africa. Under heroic efforts, the white Rhodesians built up this beautiful country three times the size of England, but they seemed to have made too little effort to really understand the thinking and feeling of their black co-citizens. One African put it in a nutshell when he said, "The whites don't know us." Then he added, "But we know them."

Family life work is a good yardstick to measure mutual understanding. Even among the churches this whole dimension seemed to be underdeveloped. Although abortion was still forbidden by law, the distribution and use of artificial contraception in order to reduce the black birth rate was only too generous: tubes tied after childbirth, pills passed out, I.U.D.s inserted, and the dangerous three month injection, Depo-Provera, given as a contraceptive under the pretext that it would help in the production of the mother's milk.

This irresponsible and light-handed dealing with black lives was paid for with the killing of white lives: "Do not be deceived . . . for whatever a man sows, that he will also reap." The Marxist-trained forces who brought down the civilian plane and killed the survivors are also partly supported by grants from the World Council of Churches (WCC) for so-called "humanitarian purposes." We realized anew the utter confusion that reigns and also to what extent the Church, and with her all of us, is involved in the death harvest of the world.

A decisive difference between the situation in Cameroun in 1958 and the fight in Rhodesia in 1978 was clearly the anti-missionary and anti-Christian thrust. It took the form of persecution of Christians in the villages. Christians did not dare to attend services and were forced to burn their Bibles or be burned alive in their huts by the black "freedom fighters." At least eight black pastors had been killed in the months just before our visit, and many others were "missing." At an English mission station in Umtali, close to the Mozambique border, nine missionaries and four children were massacred.

Recently the headlines in the Rhodesian papers announced the arrival of an American war veteran from Vietnam—called a "missionary" and gripped by "crusade" thinking—who intended to head a force of 300 military trained volunteers from the United States to defend mission stations by arms. This rightist "evangelical" sowing to the flesh is even more dangerous and deadly than the leftist sowing to the flesh of the WCC.

The National Christian Leadership Assembly (NACLA), to which we were invited in Salisbury, counteracted boldly this sowing in the flesh by a clear sowing in the Spirit: "But he who sows to the Spirit will from the Spirit reap eternal life." The whole conference was a ten-day festival of this kind of sowing.

In such a tense political situation you can imagine the risks involved in organizing this meeting where 600 people of both races—predominately black—gathered at the University of Rhodesia. Great danger was involved in just making the trip. In spite of this, they came. They sang. They prayed. They listened intently to God's word—and to each other.

No one could give a political answer. No one could offer a human solution. The testimony of this fellowship in the Spirit was simply that without any human reason for hope, an atmosphere of hope encircled all of us. A song of praise, knowing that the harvest of eternal life will certainly be brought in, rose out of the depth of desperation.

This was not an attempt, however, to escape reality. On the contrary, the participants faced reality as only Christians can. It enabled them to get their perspectives straight, separating the important from the nonimportant, preparing them for suffering in this world.

African Christians who had escaped from Uganda had a prophetic message to share from their own experience of suffering. Out of 300,000,000 Africans, 100,000,000 were already Christians at that time. If the churches continue to grow at that rate, Africa could very well become the continent with the highest percentage of Christian inhabitants. Parallel to this growth and intertwined under the surface is a constant growth of persecution. The conscious preparation for the testimony of suffering under hostile governments and persecution was the secret topic of the conference.

For many months Christians all over Rhodesia had been meeting at 5:00 A.M. to pray for their country. They believed that what God does in Rhodesia could be an example, a signal of light for all of Africa. Black and white, brothers and sisters listened to each other and embraced each other in an active reconciliation—seeds of the Spirit which will never stop growing.

There is a growing awareness of Christian family life in the churches of Africa today. We were invited to this leadership conference because of our message on Christian family life. Each delegate was given two of our books. We saw again the importance of the ministry of writing. How often we have heard, "The missionaries have taught us to read. Then the communists gave us books." We were convinced anew that our ministry filled a real gap and offered help at a very sensitive spot.

So you see, in spite of all human perplexity, the waters

of the love of God are plunging down unceasingly and in the sound of the falling waters is the voice of the Lord (Rv 1:15).

Be not deceived. God is not mocked. But he is not stingy either.

11

Teshager

TESHAGER IS AN AMHARIC WORD. It means to cross over, pass through, or bridge over. Is this not a picture of our whole lives, between birth and death, resurrection and Second Coming? Are we not always standing on the border, our hearts trembling and dismayed as we hear the command, "Cross over!"?

Teshager. Joshua 1:2 says "Cross this Jordan"—this river on the boundary line, on the border between two countries where there's no place to live, no settlement. It's a command to pack up and get ready for the new, for being "on the way."

Every trip to Africa was for us like a crossing over the Jordan. When we became older, the fast change of climate also became more strenuous for us. We had to struggle with depression and the feeling of hopelessness. We could not build upon past experiences, for each new ministry called us to rise up and cross over into new territory.

When conducting family life seminars in Ethiopia, our

close friend, brother, counselor, and interpreter was Getahun T. Getahun. Because of his deep Christian faith and his practical training as a graduate of Gondor Medical College, he was a valuable helper and advisor in our work. In November, 1973, he married our Austrian co-worker Linde Danzer, a step which was in many ways a *teshager*—crossing cultural, national, and geographical borders. It was a step taken only after much prayer and searching for guidance.

When they were married at Addis Ababa in November 1973, I used Joshua 1:9 for my message: "Be strong and of good courage! Be not frightened, neither be dismayed; for the Lord your God is with you wherever you go."

On December 9, 1974, a son was born to the Getahuns; they named him Joshua Teshager Getahun. Joshua means, "The Lord has saved."

The Getahuns have received training and practice in one *teshager* after another since they joined hands in marriage. They experienced the political change in Ethiopia, the fall of the emperor, and the taking over of power by a socialistic military government. They went through all the fears and uncertainties which are part of living in a totalitarian state. For two years, Mr. Getahun was the director of the Ethiopian Bible Society. But then he stood together with Linde before a new *teshager*.

One day out of the blue, the Getahuns were approached by U.S. AID who suggested that they start a Family Counseling Center in cooperation with the Lutheran Church in Addis Ababa. We supported them in facing this challenge and in seeking God's guidance. There were many ups and downs which followed, struggles, setbacks and disappointments, and then again surprising fulfillments of prayer and new visions for the future.

On May 29, 1976, Mr. Getahun resigned from his good job. It was a great step of faith because at that time no exit visas were being issued at all by the Ethiopian Government. One day, when they faced discouragement and uncertainty in a special way, their little son, Joshua Teshager, pointed to his mother's Bible. She gave it to him, he opened it, skimmed over the lines with his small finger, stopped, and asked his father to read. The passage was Joshua 3:7-17: "Hereby you shall know that the living God is among you. . . . The waters of the Jordan shall be stopped from flowing. . . . and the people crossed. . . ."

The Getahuns sold their car, furniture, and practically everything they owned, and with the money they bought their plane ticket to the United States via Austria. The exit visa was granted miraculously. On August 25, 1976, they arrived safely at Salzburg airport. Right there in the arrival hall, Mr. Getahun asked us and Linde's family to form a circle and share in his moving prayer of praise and thanksgiving.

We praise God that all our human *teshagers* are only an answer to his great *teshager*-call to us at Christmas and Calvary. He crossed the Jordan and bridged the gap between God and man and picks us up where we are. Therefore, we trust him and have hope as he walks side by side with us in all our human *teshagers*.

12

Re-wed after Twenty-three Years of Marriage

AFTER CONDUCTING SIX FAMILY LIFE SEMINARS in Papua, New Guinea, and in the United States, Ingrid and I felt urgently the need for some input, some work on our own marriage. We were invited to attend a weekend called Marriage Encounter. This was a wholesome experience. Twenty couples ranging from newlyweds to grandparents took part and encountered each other.

Three couples took turns introducing each session and reported in a very personal but disciplined way how they had worked at their own marriages and had deepened their relationships. At each session, we were given a list of questions. The wives went to their rooms, the men outside or to the library. Separately each couple had to write down the answers to each question. After twenty minutes, a bell rang as a signal for the husbands to join their wives. Each partner had to share the written answers and then talk together until the next bell rang and the group met again. This time another of the three leading couples introduced the topic and we received new questions. This went on unceasingly for forty-four hours, except for a few hours of sleep at night.

It was tiring, often painful, but tremendously healing. At the end we had talked longer and deeper with each other than during the whole year. We had been "encountered," and we realized how shallow our own dialogue had become. It was good to be forced to sit with each other and to say to each other, "Do you understand what you are reading?"

Writing down the answers proved to be very helpful. You have to face what the other is feeling. You cannot escape it because it is written down. You are surprised to see what comes out in formulating answers to such questions as:

Why do I want to go on living?
Why do I want to go on living with you?
What do you have to put up with in me and I in you?
What are my strong points, my weaknesses as a husband, father, Christian and as a wife, mother, Christian?

The weekend closed with the renewal of our wedding vows. In front of a simple altar, each couple was invited to repeat their promises to each other. Afterwards we were led into a festive room where a huge wedding cake awaited us. In this way, after twenty-three years we celebrated our wedding again. It is good to remember that the story which begins with the invitation, "Come up and sit with me," ends with the testimony, "He went on his way rejoicing" (Acts 8:39).

Part Three

Our Home
Remains Secret

1

Belonging Together and Yet Independent

WHEN WE WERE STILL LIVING AS A FAMILY in Cameroun, we had to send our oldest daughter to the boarding school for missionary children, almost four hundred miles from our home. I was able to visit Katrine for a few days at her school, and I wrote the following lines in my journal:

"Midday siesta. Outside a hot wind blows across the steppes. Cooking and boiling, the wind sounds exactly like a burning fire in a tile stove on a winter day. The cool atmosphere of this room breathes the same shelteredness as a heated room does on a cold day.

"As I awake I am not alone. Next to me my child's fresh and short breathing flows deep and regularly. The way she is sleeping makes me feel good. She is living and growing. In comparison to the sound of the deadening wind, her breathing is as clear as a fresh, bubbling spring.

"She raises her head, sees me, smiles, and falls back into the pillow again. She repeats this several times, but then she gets out of bed. She smiles and says nothing. There are only two expressions on her face: the seriousness of being absorbed when she is making her bed, eating, doing her homework—and this smile.

"She looks at the page I've written. She studies it. Then she smiles as if she wants to participate, to understand a part of me. She picks up a pencil and in deep concentration begins to draw hearts, many hearts. The dark golden hair, which she is letting grow so that she can have braids, falls forward and almost covers her face.

"The child cries. The ugly wart on her heel should be taken off. She complains softly, but her hand rests firmly in mine as we walk together to the hospital. Her confidence is greater than her fear.

"She refuses to lie down on the operating table. Her head cuddled on my chest, she sits up without flinching and observes the doctor's hand: the inserting of the needle for the local anesthesia—five or six times—the cutting of the scalpel, the sewing up of the incision. The unknown has given way to the known. There are no more tears. From her place of shelteredness she looks out onto that which is hostile and foreign. We are completely one and belong together. As we go back, she strides like a heroine, victoriously joyful.

"This is life: this togetherness in quietness and joy with nothing happening, at least nothing you can put your finger on. Why do we think such times don't count? Why do we really live only on the days we steal from our work?

" 'I don't care if you go now. You've been here long enough,' she tells me on the evening of the third day. This belonging together and yet independent—how wonderful!"

2

A Telegram

THE AFRICAN PASTOR AND BISHOP OF HIS CHURCH Dr. Roland Payne picked me up in Monrovia after my flight from East Africa. He had a lot of papers in his hands which meant work for me to do. The nicest of all was a telegram: "Arrived Lichtenberg all well love Ingrid."

Thanks be to God. This gave me strength for the lecture the next day at the university and for the beginning of a new seminar the following week.

3

"Whoever Would Be Great among You"

MY MOTHER WAS SUFFERING from a serious heart disease, but the doctor agreed that she could come home from the hospital and be with us. She was confined to her bed and totally dependent on us to care for her. She had an oxygen tank by her bed and one of us was always close by. Often she was at death's door. Our village doctor came to check on her daily and to give us instructions for her care.

In spite of her suffering, we had many things to be thankful for and reasons to be happy. What a wonderful plan of God that we were now in Austria and not in Africa, so we were able to give my mother the best possible care. She more than deserved this after all the sacrifices she had made during her life. We were glad that we could show her our appreciation in her time of need.

Caring for her was our most important duty, just as was the care of our children. They needed us more and more each day. Maybe God asked us purposely to do these little duties of tending my mother and the children.

We could not give a message about marriage and family to Africa and at the same time sacrifice our own marriage and family life.

Through many signs, letters, and visits we were led to the understanding that the most important thing we could do at that time was to serve the individuals of this world. The fruits of this service may be invisible at first but in the end are very promising. "Whoever would be great among you must be your servant" (Mt 20:26).

4

A Special Combination

EVERY INVITATION THAT WE ACCEPTED and ministry that we did showed us again and again that the most fruitful form of our ministry consisted in working together as a couple with a limited number of couples for several days at a time. The future of marriage counseling points in this direction—in couples helping couples.

We believe there are five parts to the special combination which we have learned over the past years and which has proven effective in helping healthy marriages grow:

1. A personal talk with each couple using the Taylor-Johnson Temperament Analysis as a tool for understanding each other.

2. Plain and understandable biblical and psychological teaching, which we learned to do in Africa.

3. Sharing the research of pioneers in natural family planning to teach couples fertility awareness and the advantages of natural birth regulation.

4. Educating fathers as well as mothers to become emotionally and physically involved in childbirth and emotionally involved in the subsequent breastfeeding.

5. The dynamics of "couple-power" gained out of the sufferings and struggles of our own marriage.

We thank our five courageous children that we could do this work together as a couple. They made no small sacrifice in order that we could build up our worldwide ministry as a team. Because they had to stand up often under the fears of separation and distance, whenever possible and when we could arrange it through discount fares, we tried to take one of them with us on our trips.

5

Ruth, Homemaker and Mother

THE MOTHER IS THE HUB of the turning wheel of her family. When she is not feeling well and is "off-balance," the whole family seems to suffer with her, even if she carries the burden of her illness courageously.

Recently we had great joy in the visit of the African bishop of the Liberian Lutheran church, Dr. Roland Payne. Since his return flight to Monrovia was already booked up, he had to stay four days longer than he had planned. Ingrid and I were scheduled for a seminar. We had no other choice but to leave the African bishop with our children. Stephen was in charge of fixing breakfast, Ruth was responsible for lunch, and Daniel for supper. On Sunday morning the bishop held an unforgettable Sunday service for the children. He later wrote that Ruth, housekeeper and mother, took care of him just as if Ingrid herself had been there.

If we are asked how parents can make their children become believers, we have to reply: You can't. This can only happen through the grace of God. Ingrid would say, "One has to give birth to a child over and over again. You have to cut the umbilical cord repeatedly in order to give them complete freedom and risk everything on God." While it is possible to talk to your children about God, it is more important to talk to God about them. Faith does not happen by using forceful means, not even through good advice or well-intended protection; it only happens through his Spirit whose presence cannot be forced on anyone.

6

Our Oldest Daughter Gets Married

WE ONLY HAD A FEW DAYS after our return from Liberia before we left for Boston to attend the wedding of our oldest daughter Katrine to David Stewart and to witness their courageous crossing over into the new land of marriage.

Their wedding on Pentecost Sunday, June 6, 1976, was the simplest we had ever experienced. They wanted the whole congregation present, so the ceremony was just a part of the regular Sunday morning worship service of the church where David has been an active member during his student years. We found it all very meaningful—no bridesmaids, best man, wedding march, or walking down the aisle. Katrine wore the simple white wedding dress her mother had made in Africa for her own wedding twenty-five years earlier.

As their parents, we talked over with them the problems of such an early marriage—they were both twenty-one and still students at Harvard and Wellesley. We respected their decision, especially since it was meant as a testimony.

"So few student couples get married that what we are doing is almost a novelty," they told us. "Although most of our non-Christian friends think nothing of living together, they don't have the courage to make a final decision and get married. The choice of our style of life which makes no compromise is a powerful message for these friends."

We would like to add: "Love rejoices in the truth!" A halfway decision carries with it dishonesty and even injustice. We rejoice with this young couple.

7

At Mother's Death Bed
Easter 1967

D EATH IS NOT PLEASANT. It is not the poets who celebrate death in song who are right, but the Bible that calls death the last enemy to be conquered.

"When someone is dying, everything else takes second place," our friend said to us as we took turns watching at the bedside of my mother. This was a redeeming word for us. Didn't we do the same thing when our children were born? Do we give death a lesser place? When we stopped trying to do our normal work in addition to nursing my mother, we became more relaxed and free.

During the last night between 12:00 and 3:00 A.M., our friend was at Mother's bedside. Then I took over. Mother still recognized me and smiled at me. When I asked her if she was thirsty, she nodded. Every time I called out the name "Jesus" to her, her eyes lit up. She could not talk anymore. After her coughing spell I gave her the medicine prescribed by the doctor. She soon fell asleep. I put the oxygen mask on her which made it easier for her to breathe. Because of the soft whistling noise, I could not determine exactly when she took her last breath. She calmly passed away without opening her eyes again. It must have been around 6:45 A.M.

When we opened the drapes and looked out through the window, we saw a clear, bright morning. The snow-covered summits of the nearby mountains shone in the morning sun, a foretaste of the resurrection morning: "I want to know him and the power of his resurrection."

We experienced an unforgettable hour with the children at their grandmother's deathbed. They asked many questions which were not easy to answer: "Where is she now?" "Can she see us?" "Will we see her again?" Afterwards we heard five-year-old Ruth say to seven-year-old Stephen, "I want to die too; then I can be with Jesus!" "Unless you become like children. . . ."

Upon my mother's request, I held the memorial service in our village. She had chosen the text before her death: "For our citizenship is in heaven, and from it we await a Savior, the Lord Jesus Christ" (Phil 3:20).

My mother was a very down-to-earth person, and for her it was difficult to adjust to the reality of the world of God's Kingdom. Again and again, to the amazement of her physicians, she overcame the crises of her illness with her strong will to live. We witnessed, however, how she slowly gave in and was more and more willing to suffer. Her pastor greatly helped her in this acceptance. We celebrated Holy Communion with her several times. She was by nature a joyful and happy person, and she remained so until the night of her death when she experienced joyful anticipation: "I want to know him and the power of his resurrection." When she was finally released from her long suffering, her fine, sensitive features were transformed by this joy and the new beauty of the heavenly person.

As hard as it is to deal with death's finality and mercilessness, it is a great help in gaining the right perspective on that which is important and that which is not important. Are we able to concentrate on the last reality which awaits us in all of our hunting and struggling? In the end, only two things are important: "to know him"—this means meeting him—and then to live out "the power of his resurrection."

In preparing for both my Advent and Easter sermons, it became clear to me again that our faith is totally dependent on our personal meeting with the coming one and the resurrected one. Only from this aspect does everything fall into place. If this meeting does not take place, we are avoiding the issue. Doesn't all the discussion of the so-called modern theology really center around this one question: Does such a personal encounter really exist? It is not the one who throws out the most questions who is a great theologian, but the one who can answer the children's questions about death!

And where does the power to do this come from? There is so much advice given today in deep books about marriage and life counseling, but if someone asks where to get the strength to carry out this advice, the experts keep silent. Today more is expected from psychoanalysis than from the power of the resurrection. Whoever dares to offer this resurrection power as a real help to face life problems will get no more than a benevolent smile today. Both in the church and outside of the church, this is considered unscientific and old-fashioned. When facing death, we don't want to lose sight of the goal for which alone it is worthwhile both to live and to die: "I want to know him and the power of his resurrection."

8

Birth and Death
March 1977

O N CHRISTMAS EVE, the Getahuns were given a daughter, Verena Tesfa (Hope), and little Joshua was given a sister. The father was allowed to be present at the birth so he could share this precious experience of marriage with Linde. When they left the hospital, the proud and thankful father held his daughter in both arms and singing "hallelujah" walked up the stairs to their fourth floor apartment in Salzburg.

In between the birth and baptism of Verena Tesfa was the death of our dear neighbor Theresia Eichhorn, a retired farmer's widow also known as Resltant. She was a grandmother not only for her own grandchildren but also for our children. To us she became a loving mother who faithfully supported us in prayer.

We were deeply touched in this rural Austrian community by how people are more aware of what it means to die. Death is not pushed out into the anonymity of a hospital. Those last weeks of Resltant's life were almost like a celebration when death had priority over everyday life. Almost every day I sat at her bedside and prayed with her. Neighbors and relatives from far and near came to bid farewell, and Resltant wanted to see them all.

We shall never forget the last time we celebrated Holy Communion with her. Both her children and grandchildren took part, all of them fully aware that the end was near. But just this awareness created a relaxed atmosphere which even let happiness seep in. To lie to the dying about his true condition up until the last moment is inhuman and only makes everyone poorer. We were richly endowed at this hour. We can see how a person has lived by how he dies. When we forget how to live, we also forget how to die.

2

Deathwake

AFTER RESLTANT'S DEATH, all the family members and neighbors gathered together in the big living room of the farmhouse to keep "the wake." This is an Austrian custom at which time the singing of hymns and the reading of the Scripture are performed alternately; death and life are honored and celebrated in word and song. On this occasion, an atmosphere prevailed which was both sober and yet full of praise, far from pathos and mourning. Both Catholic and Protestant friends came together at this occasion.

The next day, after the funeral, they all came together for a simple meal at a nearby restaurant. Without any fuss, the connection to everyday life was again established. There are probably not many places in the world today where one may die in such a way.

Afterword
When Morning Came, Jesus Stood on the Shore

The Lord is near to the brokenhearted (Ps 34:18).

Our beloved father was called home on the morning of October 13, 1979, just ten days after he returned to Austria from a teaching trip around the world. He had gotten up early as usual and had gone on his morning run through the woods of the Lichtenberg. Then, in his caring and loving way, he brought Mother a tray with early morning tea into the bedroom. Moments later he died of a heart attack. We are deeply moved and our hearts are saddened because of his sudden departure from our midst. In this letter we want to share as his children the closeness of God that we have experienced during the last days. Not only through prayer but also through loving friends, he spoke to us. We include some of these words from your letters as well as from the messages at Father's graveside.

But when morning came, Jesus stood on the shore (Jn 21:4).

These words are engraved on Father's tombstone where he lies buried next to his mother in the churchyard in Attersee. Father loved the morning and if it ever happened that he got up after sunrise, he was dissatisfied with himself. How often for him did Jesus stand on the shore in the early morning hours. How often did he call him aloud by his name! One of Father's favorite texts was Mark 1:35: "And in the morning, a great while before day, he arose and went out to a lonely place, and there he prayed." Early in his life, Father was called by Jesus to throw out the net into the sea of nations. The net was the biblical message on Christian marriage and the family. He lived true to his commission.

He died in the morning. Jesus called him home at his most treasured time of the day. The eternal morning dawned. "We find it significant that he literally ran to the end of his life," one of you wrote. Yes, he ate quickly, worked quickly, slept quickly, and died quickly. After a packed life of only fifty-five years, he has now won the race. "His path did not lead into the darkness, but into the day. Not into obscurity, but into light. Not away from, but very close to the Lord." We praise the Lord for this.

"Where do we go? Always homeward!"

These were the words that Father wrote above the itinerary of his last trip.

Father will always remain in my memory as a "traveler." Especially when I was younger, it was one of the hardest things for me to see him and Mother leave. But in the moment we were all back together again it seemed as if all the waiting, all the longing and the feeling of being left behind was completely blotted out. I can well remember how he asked me once what would make me happy. I said, "The coming back home." His answer: "How can you come back home if you have not been away from home?"

Stephen, 19, first year at
Institute of Technology, Vienna

Now he is at home. Jesus may have prepared him a meal just as he did for his disciples that morning at the water's edge, and they are celebrating together. How Father liked to celebrate with us here on earth. Even out of the most trivial occasions, he could make feasts of Joy.

Father provided so well for us and was always concerned about how he could give us the best, both spiritually and physically. Our well-being was always more important to him than his own. One of the last things he did with Mother was to make decisions about the arrangements for our higher education. With tears in my eyes, I raise my head and wonder at how I could so often take his generosity for granted.

Father put his whole soul into it when he planned for his family. He always tried to plan the right thing at the right time at the right place. Woe then, if things did not work out as planned! It's almost now as if my aching heart feels him making arrangements for us in heaven. . . ."

Katrine Stewart, mother of two and homemaker in Richmond, Virginia

Although Father died early, he left us much to remember him by. Through his letters and books we will be close to him for many more years. He made our lives and the lives of many others rich. We thank him. As one of our friends has said, "Walter is not only living among us in spirit but also is in communication with us through his magnificent books and his burning spirit of love and care as one of the dynamic soldiers of Christ."

Perhaps, as the eldest son, after having worked closely with him during these last years, I was the most conscious—even before his death—of the intellectual and spiritual inheritance of my father. A wonderful treasure of immeasurable wealth and a tremendous responsibility!

That is why I daily pray for grace to be able to grow more intimately into union with our heavenly Father and Provider. One day I hope to pass on to my children and grandchildren what my beloved father has given me.

Daniel, 23, postgraduate student in psychology, University of Salzburg

At the funeral service, Pastor Endres said, "Walter has again taken the first step as he has gone before us in so many ways." God will help us to bear the sad burden of our loss. The whole load which Father carried will divide itself up into smaller loads. Mother will just have to make one decision at a time, and she knows where to find the strength to do it.

Here are some words from the letter that Father wrote me for my eighteenth birthday on September 12. "Anxiety and tension hover over your eighteenth birthday as you read the Watchword: 'Who can stand when He appears?' (Mal 3:2) and James 2:13, 'For judgment is without mercy to one who has shown no mercy.' The urgent content of this word will not help you to be relaxed, but the word 'mercy' radiates over all. In German, *Barmherzigkeit* (mercy) means to carry with your heart. This is almost a life-program for your 'coming of age.' I do not know what your future will look like. The secret, though, of a fulfilled life is that you let yourself be carried by the heart of God. And from there you can then gain strength to carry others with your heart."

Anxiety and tension have really hovered over these last days since Father's death, but we all have experienced over and over again the *Barmherzigkeit* (the mercy) of God. I would like to take as the motto for my future these words which Father wrote in my devotional book for the year 1979: "God always shows us just the next step."

Ruth, 18, preparing for her university
entrance exams at a Salzburg Gymnasium

God's unfathomable mercy clearly showed us the next step after Father's funeral on October 18. Together with our friends and close relatives we witnessed the baptism of his second grandchild, Virginia Ruth Stewart, in our little home on the Lichtenberg, with Ruth as her godmother.

Virginia was the last person Father gave a blessing to before he left the United States October 2. We know that he was with us in spirit. In one of his last German newsletters, telling about the death of one of our neighbors here, he wrote: "Birth and death embraced each other. We experienced the reality of both since they have their origin in God in a strange and surprising harmony and peace."

In the hours just before my birth in Ebolowa, Cameroun, Father wrote the following lines in the journal Mother had begun for me:

"We can only understand the Exile. *Our home remains secret.* The more we feel it, the more mysterious it becomes. The foreign becomes home and what is home becomes foreign to us. Messenger from Home—you are coming into your Exile! Why? May you become a messenger, be a messenger, bring the Home into your Exile! May you not get lost in your exile, but find your way back on the joyful day of your return.

"Which day is greater—the one of birth or the one of death? Why are both days necessary?

"We do not know. Light is only at one spot—at that point where God went the same way that you are going today. We are never alone."

David, 21, fourth year student of theology at University of Heidelberg

Christ remains on the shore even if his servant goes on. He waits for us and is the only one given to us from God as the answer to all our questions, problems, and needs, even in the darkness of the night. A blessing once given to Mother and Father was:

"As children of the Father, we can run to him, weep, stammer, rest, and be set free by the Father. The Father is more merciful than we can imagine, and the Son leads on. . . ."

"May the voice that silenced the waves of old Galilee calm us now in this hour of distress and keep us in the loving memory of the one who has ended his sojourn here to be with the Father" (Bishop Payne of Liberia).

Other Books of Interest
from Servant Publications

Learning to Walk Alone
Personal Reflections on a Time of Grief
By Ingrid Trobisch

In this touching memoir, Ingrid Trobisch shares about how she dealt with the sudden death of her beloved husband Walter. She provides counsel, encouragement, and hope for anyone who knows what it means to lose a loved one. (hardcover) *$8.95*

A Lamp for My Feet
Reflections on Life with God
By Elisabeth Elliot

Insightful reflections on Scripture from one of today's most respected Christian authors. (hardcover) *$9.95*

Chosen Vessels
Portraits of Ten Outstanding Christian Men
Edited by Charles Turner

Ten of today's Christian leaders write candidly about their heroes. Essays by Malcolm Muggeridge (on Alexander Solzhenitsyn), Harry Blamires (on C.S. Lewis), and others. Thoroughly enjoyable reading. (hardcover) *$10.95*

Available at your Christian bookstore or from:
Servant Publications • Dept. 209 • P.O. Box 7455
Ann Arbor, Michigan 48107
Please include payment plus $.75 per book
for postage and handling.
Send for our FREE catalog of Christian
books, music, and cassettes.